PERFORMANCE MANAGEMENT AND APPRAISAL

IN HEALTH SERVICES

MARTIN EDIS

Working together for Health

KOGAN
PAGE

First published in 1995

Kogan Page Limited
120 Pentonville Road
London N1 9JN

British Library Cataloguing in Publication Data

A CIP record for this book is available from the British Library.

ISBN 0 7494 1731 5

Typeset by Kogan Page
Printed and bound in Great Britain by
Biddles Ltd, Guildford and King's Lynn

Contents

NAHAT

NAHAT (National Association of Health Authorities and Trusts) is the leading organisation working for NHS management bodies. It brings together NHS authorities, health boards and NHS trusts into one representative organisation covering the separate and collective views of both purchasers and providers. It represents members' interests to Ministers and to other decision-makers. It promotes the benefits of the NHS and provides its members with a wide range of support services, research, conferences and publications as an aid to the delivery of high-quality healthcare.

Preface

In every walk of life and in every sort of venture, it is the people who make up organisations that impact most strongly on the quality of the product or service for which that organisation exists. Given that people are much the same the world over, why is it that some organisations are more successful than others? It may simply be that the people who work within them are performing better.

In the NHS, staff, whose pay accounts for 70 per cent of all the costs incurred on health in this country, are a particularly precious asset. The chief executive of the largest acute trust, all the clinical, nursing and other care groups, medical records clerks, estates managers and hospital porters – everyone has a direct impact on the quality of care given to patients. Each therefore needs to realise his or her full potential, and to feel they are playing a real part in improving the health of the nation.

A big step towards achieving this is the effective performance management and appraisal of each staff member. I believe the very practical guidance in this book will be invaluable to all those in the NHS seeking to enhance individual performance and overall quality. It covers areas such as performance-related pay, which is of current concern in the NHS, alongside in-depth advice on appraisal, objective setting and review. Every single manager in the NHS needs to take these messages on board; I commend this book as a really useful support tool in this vital area.

Philip Hunt
Director, NAHAT

Series Editor's Foreword

'Fitter, leaner organisations' has been the catch-phrase for the process of removing layers of middle managers from NHS organisations. For senior managers this has meant either taking on more work and facing personal burnout or delegating tasks and authority to staff who have not worked as managers in the past and who do not usually feel trained to do so.

The Health Care Management series is aimed at just such people: operational staff such as heads of department or localities in purchasing or provider organisations, ward sisters/charge nurses and their deputies who find that they are increasingly expected to deal with management issues which, until only recently, they were expected to refer upwards.

To complicate matters further, such delayering of our organisations has come at a time of the most radical alterations to the systems for planning, commissioning and delivering healthcare since the service was founded. The National Health Service seems rapidly to be turning into the 'National Health Business' with an ethos and methods that feel alien to many of the staff expected to live with them. The boundaries between health and social services become ever more blurred as care is increasingly delivered in or near to clients' own homes, upsetting established patterns of working just as new and inexperienced managers take over the reins. The new organisations that have formed are undergoing a period of rapid learning and team building to undertake their new roles.

One of the key aspects of working in the Health Service is that it is fundamentally a process of people caring for other people. There is virtually no automation of caring (apart from data processing) and little scope for it! As a result, the quality and efficiency of the service is entirely dependent upon the skills of our staff and our deployment of them. Virtually the only way to achieve significant improvement in the service is through the better use of staff. On the other hand, poor staff management, training and motivation are probably the most frequent cause of breakdowns in service quality and safety so that their maintenance becomes the prime concern of operational managers.

It seems that there are so many techniques for appraisal, objective setting and staff motivation that the field is becoming very confusing and many of us wonder what to do for the best. This book aims to get to the core of what is important and what actually helps healthcare professionals and support workers to do a better job. It offers practical advice to managers on how to get the most from staff appraisals.

Subsequent titles will reflect the general issues affecting all managerial or supervisory staff, as well as throwing light on the changes to healthcare in the UK to which they must respond. The authors have been chosen for their practical experience of dealing with these issues themselves, or of helping others to do so. The books in this series are therefore not academic treatises but working handbooks full of advice and practical aids. We hope that they will prove to be useful tools in the rapid personal development that will be needed.

Keith Holdaway
Assistant Director Human Resources
Mayday Healthcare NHS Trust, Surrey
1995

Chapter 1

Welcome to the Circus: Approaches to Performance Management

It's Performance that Counts

Healthcare management is everywhere undergoing unprecedented change. With staff costs making up 70 per cent of the total budget, and more and more competitiveness in service quality and productivity, effective use of staff resources to achieve high levels of performance has become a crucial management objective. To match a competitive healthcare market, the government and NHS Executive have sought to encourage a more competitive and integrated approach to managing performance, pay and rewards.

There is now scope for importing management ideas that have had little previous application in the NHS, with its reliance on nationally negotiated and funded pay and rigid job demarcations. Now, the way professional staff are used and rewarded is under review. Work roles are being restructured to make greater use of unqualified staff. Performance review and reward management are being energetically promoted as a means of enhancing performance. The result is a confusing circus display of pay-scale acrobatics, trial-and-error introductions of new performance management systems, and resuscitation of appraisal.

In a competitive environment, the ability for managers to influence staff performance is fundamental to success. Performance issues can no longer be taken for granted. Suddenly there is more flexibility and opportunity, through performance management, to generate significant improvements from which patients can benefit.

At present staff morale is said to be low and stress levels are high. Many professionals in health services are still unsure about their response to the new management agenda which emphasises competitiveness and effective management of resources while ignoring some traditional concerns. Some find the new language baffling. While they understand the need to respond to change and demonstrate their ability to contribute to business objectives, they want to be sure that the culture that emerges incorporates their values and goes beyond simply jumping through contractual hoops.

This new management style is still developing. It will need to concern itself with more than imposing output and efficiency targets. Professional standards, together with development and support for staff, must be included. Staff will not respond to performance regimes where they have to struggle to achieve the most basic care standards with a background of over-stretched resources and insecurity about their future. Trust, and a sense of common purpose, must be consciously developed.

The idea of managing performance is here to stay. Healthcare managers need to understand what is happening and know what responses to make. This requires them to be involved in business plans and to work with staff to create objectives that meet performance demands without sacrificing important values. Managers must know what they want from appraisal schemes, and ensure that they and their staff have sufficient control over the processes.

What this Book Covers

This book contains discussions of performance management, staff motivation and performance pay in a health services management context. Specific guidance is offered on performance appraisal and objective-setting, including examples of a personal achievement plan that includes personal development and performance review.

This first chapter introduces performance management and some of the approaches to it. Chapter 2 looks at its application to healthcare, its role in supporting current management priorities, and its impact on traditional clinical professions. Chapter 3 describes the links between effort, performance and personal outcomes, which are important to an understanding of the performance management model based on expectancy theory. This is supplemented by consideration of other motivation theories.

The practical requirements for maximising achievement are the subject of Chapter 4. Managers can compare their own management style to the requirements.

The basic stages and processes of formal and informal staff appraisal are explained in Chapter 5. Advice is given on how to make appraisal meetings successful and rewarding for both parties as a means of improving performance, developing staff and getting their commitment. Chapter 6 explains the competences required in appraisal, including those of giving feedback, performance assessment, delegation, supporting staff and problem solving. Chapter 7 explains how to write individual performance standards and objectives in an organisational context. Chapter 8 relates objectives to jobs, and Chapter 9 is about writing development objectives which are later incorporated into individual achievement plans responding to corporate, service and individual needs. Chapter 10 provides a case study of performance review and discusses appraisal tactics. Chapter 11 is a critical review of performance related pay and its implications for managers.

Components of Performance Management

The Need

Performance management comes about, as Alan Fowler (1990) says, because there is no guarantee that all managers in an organisation will work to a coherent set of goals and priorities, or that they will consistently achieve the standards required. In a broad sense, the term refers to any integrated, systematic approach to improving organisational performance to achieve an organisation's strategic aims and promote its mission and values.

The Philosophy

So we might need to start with a *philosophy* (to which everyone can subscribe) endorsing the achievement of certain goals throughout the whole organisation. Since most human beings enjoy being productive, and enjoying the rewards from their successes, it is not difficult to sell people the idea of achievement. However, to go beyond empty platitudes and bring everyone on board, the achievement must be in strategically important areas, and based on a common sense of mission or purpose.

An Achievement Culture

The rather ugly term *performance orientation* describes a culture where there is a general concern for meeting targets for turnover or profit, quality or customer satisfaction. Although these can be translated into healthcare terms, most professionals would also want to recognise a broader basis of achievement than simply meeting the employer's performance targets. This would put patient care at the centre of things and recognise professional obligations and personal needs as well as meeting corporate objectives. Achievement for the healthcare professional is accomplishing results for patients, the organisation, the profession, co-workers and oneself. Hence in this book an *achievement culture* means a combination of performance orientation and professional excellence.

The Management Role

Managers must be the standard-bearers of the values and mission, and agents of its accomplishment. They must have the ability and inclination to deliver. Their management style must promote achievement by them and their staff (see Chapter 4).

Processes and Systems

Formal processes will need to be put in place to support performance management and achieve a coordinated approach. We can call these processes a *performance management system* if its components are designed to integrate (see Figure 1.1). In practice they might include any or all of the following:

- strategies for performance improvement
- performance measurement, objectives and standard setting
- work analysis and job restructuring
- performance appraisal
- skills training
- coaching and counselling
- personal development plans
- performance related pay
- succession planning
- team building
- communication processes.

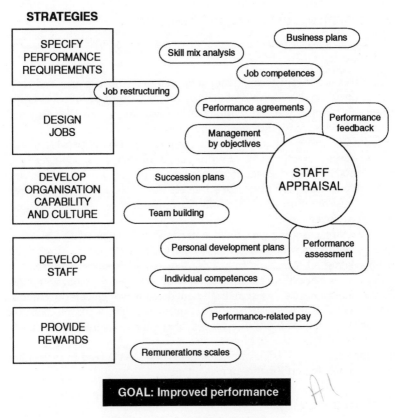

STRATEGIES

Figure 1.1 The components of performance management

Key Approaches

Feedback On Performance

Give individuals information on whether their performance is satisfactory, as a basis for maintaining and improving required standards.

Few would quarrel with the idea that people need to know how they are doing, or that there is a need to ensure that people receive information on their achievements and efforts. This may be factual feedback on results: eg it worked, or it failed. It can also involve clarifying expectations and making some assessment of where people are falling short of them. In the right climate for learning, people ask for and generate feedback themselves.

Performance Objectives and Standards

Identify and agree objectives or standards for everyone to link up with required achievements for the organisation.

Objectives are useful because they link well to business plans, and they can be long- or short-term and be changed as current priorities change. They can be created for individuals or a whole team. Whether they are broad or very specific, they need to be linked to observable results. Not all jobs lend themselves to objective setting, and they do not provide a way of comparing directly levels of individual performance or achievement. In a period of rapid change, objectives tend to be very unstable. If we are looking to reward individuals for achieving objectives, we must remember that success or failure often has complex causes and cannot be attributed to the employee alone.

The notion of setting performance standards is fundamental – the actual ones to be used may be a matter for debate. Currently there is a move away from relating all standards to activity targets and business performance indicators, because this can drive out quality and staff development aims. Some professional staff resist management demands for greater throughput where they feel it will adversely affect quality of care. If commitment on performance standards is to be achieved, discussion and agreement on these points is vital. They need to be assessable as objectively as possible. Some will say 'the value of my work cannot be measured'. Yet agreed measures are indispensable in performance management.

Performance Appraisal

Set up discussions between managers and subordinates to provide the means of clarifying performance expectations, reviewing progress, recognising achievements and shortfalls and developing plans with the individual.

This is seen as a cornerstone of performance management. Typical past experience of schemes is not always positive. They are too cumbersome, too loaded with paperwork, create artificial deadlines and are not valued by staff or managers. A new approach to appraisal must ensure that the positive benefits are realised and that the enthusiasm of staff and managers is maintained. I deal in depth with the subject of appraisal in Chapters 5 and 6.

Performance Rating and Assessment

Measure and record level of performance, achievement, or competence.

Performance rating has moved from unreliable and unpopular subjective ratings of personality traits to either specially constructed and validated *behavioural ratings* or measures of the extent to which *objectives are achieved.* Competence assessment has recently made assessment itself into an industry. There are many problems in performance assessment, including what to measure, how to measure it and who should do so. The sensitivity of such measures requires the process to be carefully managed if it is not to lead to loss of motivation and distortions of the appraisal process (see Chapters 5 and 6). Reasons for assessment might include: to allocate people to bands for remuneration (performance pay); to identify promotable people; to select for new jobs during restructuring; to identify training requirements and development needs; or to measure and compare levels of performance.

Performance Agreements

Create a contract between manager and subordinate (or team) to achieve agreed results within a specified time with specified resources.

The origin of performance agreements is in contracting for services and in industrial relations negotiations with staff for productivity. At a time when individual contract negotiation by employees is becoming prevalent, and bonus schemes for ancillary staff are being renegotiated locally, the culture of *performance agreements* is becoming fairly widespread. More personal and informal 'contracts' or agreements between manager and staff member are very valuable. They help stimulate achievement and build relationships.

Personal Development Plans

Create a contract between manager and subordinate to resource, support and implement agreed development objectives for the subordinate.

Work can be a rich source of learning. Personal development planning can be done inside or outside the appraisal process – but a review of performance ought to provide the opportunity to diagnose needs that have emerged and anticipate the learning required to ensure the achievement of future objectives. Work assignments can be used to generate useful learning opportunities. However, many managers (and subordinates) do not consider learning opportunities other than through formal courses and education.

Job Restructuring

Analyse the currently available workforce skills in comparison to what is needed in any place and time. Then optimise the skills pattern by adjusting overall grading structures and job specifications. Review and revamp the content of jobs to ensure people use all their abilities and achieve greater productivity and job satisfaction.

This has become a growth industry within healthcare in the past few years, as managers have looked for cost savings by 'delayering' organisations and creating new 'care worker' roles requiring less competence than the qualified staff they replace. Such *workforce reprofiling* has required major organisational change. More traditional approaches include *job enrichment* where jobs are redesigned to make them more meaningful.

Competences

Identify the particular behaviour required to achieve certain outcomes and link these to performance standards and training objectives.

Although there is still some confusion about how competences differ from skills and knowledge, their introduction has created a stimulus for identifying the actual behaviour required to achieve effective performance. In this sense competence is defined most satisfactorily as the ability to achieve a measurable behavioural outcome to which a standard can be attached. This is potentially very useful. Yet the movement to establish national competency standards for a wide range jobs in the UK has not always matched the requirements of particular organisations. The more generalised (or elaborate) the statements of competence, the less likely they are to be actually relevant in any particular organisation.

Performance Related Pay (PRP)

To relate financial rewards to individual or group performance outcomes.

Pay is used as an incentive to get enhanced performance. The performance-pay element is normally a small part of total remuneration, although it needs to be large enough to be valued. It may be that bonuses are paid for meeting productivity, quality or, low sickness absence targets, or even for acquiring competences. They may be paid to teams or directorates as well as individuals. PRP is widely criticised (see Chapter 11 for an assessment).

Development-Based Performance Management

To improve performance by improving staff capability.

Instead of relying on extrinsic rewards, investment is made in the competences of staff. In a culture where learning is valued, and the work itself is seen as largely rewarding, this can be effective, because people will want to extend their own abilities and take on more challenging assignments, without necessarily seeking extra payment. This also helps to create a flexible workforce which can meet future demands more effectively. The ideal here is often called 'the learning organisation' – referring to one where work opportunities for learning are identified and deliberately maximised, to create a culture where everyone is encouraged to learn and adapt to change. This has been used by Motorola in the USA and Unipart in Great Britain. This is a strategy often contrasted with the 'pay for performance' strategy. Its disadvantage might lie in the difficulty of directing it to short-term goals, and on measuring the return on investment in training and learning activity.

Quality-Driven Performance Management

To improve performance by emphasising responsibility for quality and empowering staff to make improvements.

Quality assurance strategies have been traditionally associated with improving quality, not productivity. They are not always separable in practice – for instance, quality circles can be used as a means to improve performance and implement change locally. What is important here is the process of participation which encourages commitment and self-monitoring of results, and the *process by which ideas are implemented*. Failure here often leads to loss of staff's faith in such systems.

Expectancy Theory

In a work context, it is performance that is rewarded, not just effort. Hence people will make an effort to achieve performance provided they believe it will be rewarded by some desirable outcome. Conversely, they will be reluctant simply to 'bash their head against a brick wall', if they have learnt that the results do not bring worthwhile outcomes.

This is the theory which underpins performance management (Vroom, 1964). It explains the relationship between individual performance, effort and outcomes (or rewards), and the factors that can affect these links (see Figure 1.2). By *effort* we mean the physical and mental exertions made by the individual, whereas *performance* implies a level of effective functioning which may have little correlation with the effort expended. To enhance the link between effort and performance we must consider working conditions, equipment and training, since the lack of any of these will degrade performance, even where the effort is strong. (See Chapter 3 for a detailed analysis of these issues.)

9

Use of Rewards in Performance Management Systems

Performance management is the process of trying to the bring rewards or outcomes which *individuals* desire into line with those required by the *organisation*. We know that the range of desirable outcomes that people in healthcare jobs seek for themselves is quite wide. There will be a number of non-material (often socially rewarding) outcomes that enter the equation. Professional prestige and patient welfare would seem to be as important as perks such as extra holidays and cash incentives in motivating staff to perform well. On the other hand, there is a danger in thinking that *material* rewards can be neglected entirely, or that performance pay will never be an incentive for professional staff.

Reward-based performance management systems work by providing rewards only for desired behaviour and performance. If these do not meet requirements, then there is no reason for the organisation to reward them, and the motivational chain for the individual based on expectancy is absent. The main problem is that adverse assessments generate argument, resentment and loss of motivation.

Development-based performance management relies less on providing external rewards. Instead, individual abilities are developed through encouraging learning. Motivation is intrinsic, and will include the satisfaction to the individual of using the skills in patient care.

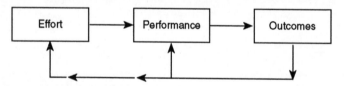

Figure 1.2 Expectancy theory

Other Approaches

Succession planning, business planning, work study, organisation development and team building are also important in performance management.

The components we have mentioned should support managers. Too often they have been seen primarily as methods of standardisation and control imposed and controlled by others outside the workplace, inhibiting local managers' control over the process. Recent reports suggest that the most successful schemes are ones which allow managers great discretion and control. They know what will work. Overall performance aims are translated into terms that are locally meaningful and people feel ownership of the process. Performance management works best if built on the right management style and motivation.

Overall Strategy

There are several important questions here:

1. To Develop Methodology or People?

The emphasis can be on establishing improved methods of work (defining best practice, clarifying work roles, quantifying tasks and standards, etc), or on giving people the chance to create their own methods of working (staff empowerment).

2. What Assumptions are to be Made about Staff Rewards And Motivation?

Will performance directly influence pay? Or will staff be motivated to achieve high performance in some other way? We cannot answer this without studying the organisational environment; Chapter 2 discusses the issues in healthcare.

Summary

A performance management system is an integrated, systematic approach to improve the results of people's efforts (ie, the means by which employees' performance can be improved by ensuring appropriate recognition and reward for their efforts, and by improving communication, learning and working arrangements).

Performance management enables an organisation to create and support the 'achievement culture' and thus to ensure that effort is generated that results in performance which in turn results in real achievements for the whole organisation. It stems from a clear understanding by everyone of the organisation's mission and values, and of what it wants to achieve. Its success depends on managers developing a style that promotes achievement and having the right motivation.

Performance management systems are designed to support managers and provide coordination. Components might include any or all of the following:

objectives that emphasise performance improvement;
performance measurement and standard setting;
staff appraisal;
skills training;
coaching and counselling;
personal development plans;
performance related pay;
succession planning;
team building; communications and feedback processes which link these together.

Key approaches in performance management include:

feedback on performance;
objectives and standard setting;
performance appraisal;
performance assessment;
performance agreements;
personal development plans;
job restructuring;
competences.

Reward-based performance management systems work by providing rewards only for desired behaviour and performance. Development-based performance management relies less on providing external rewards. Instead, individual capabilities are developed through encouraging learning.

Expectancy theory maintains that it is performance that has to be rewarded, not just effort – and that people will make an effort to achieve performance provided they believe it will be rewarded by some desirable outcome. This theory *underpins* performance management.

Chapter 2

Could do Better? Performance Management in Healthcare

This chapter explores the relevance of performance management ideas in healthcare and the impact they are likely to have on the existing culture. Traditional means for maintaining standards of performance are very influential in healthcare. Staff are recruited, trained and socialised in particular ways, and bring certain assumptions to their work, which do not always match the assumptions made by human resource specialists who are keen to introduce promising new schemes for improving performance, based on business practice. The healthcare manager charged with implementing new systems is often all too sharply aware of the divergences. In order to understand the issues and the debates, we need to start by looking at the organisational benefits claimed for performance management.

What can Performance Management do?

There is a long list of benefits claimed for performance management (see Armstrong, 1994):

- *Direct improvements in performance* can improve performance, both immediately and in the longer term. It helps organisations achieve and integrate corporate and individual objectives. Actual day-to-day performance improves.
- *Communications* will give staff a better understanding of corporate aims and priorities. New and better communication channels become available. People are more aware of what is required of them.

- *Capability* is improved by developing knowledge, skill and overall competence.
- *Organisation and staff development* helps achieve cultural and behavioural change and it welds together different parts of the organisation with different cultures. It improves staff morale and motivation for higher performance. It empowers people by giving them more control over their work and their personal development and supports total quality management. Working relations between managers and their staff are strengthened, maximising the contribution that managers and staff can make jointly to the long-term success of the organisation. It enables personal development to take place in line with organisational needs. Managerial competence develops.
- *Human resource strategy*: staff can be used effectively. Skilled staff are attracted and retained. There is a sound basis for payment by results.

The Audit Commission, in a study of local authorities in 1994, concluded that the potential benefits of performance management were not always being achieved, because of poor management. They stated three important principles for success: *specification of values and objectives; employee communication and consultation; and evaluation of outcomes.*

Many private sector organisations have introduced performance management in one form or another. There are as yet few comprehensive studies of the results. The main area of current concern seems to be the linking of performance with pay, a sensitive area, often handled badly and consequently undermining trust in the whole system. (See Chapter 11 for a fuller discussion.)

Who owns Performance Management?

Recently performance management has become a vogue word, frequently used by executives and personnel directors about grand business and human resource strategies, rather than as something that can be taken up by working managers. Michael Armstrong (1994) warns against this view:

> In essence, performance management is a shared process between managers and the individuals and teams they manage. It is based on the principle of management by contract rather than command, although this does not exclude the need to incorporate high performance expectations in such contracts... it should be regarded as a process which is driven by management so that it becomes a valued part of their everyday working life and not an annual bureaucratic chore imposed upon them by the Human Resource Department.

Personnel managers will be experts on the design and implementation of the system, and will facilitate its introduction, act as 'trouble shooters' and be in good position to monitor its effectiveness. They will also be able to ensure that other important things like job design and corporate training provision are right. However, their interest in performance management must not become proprietorial. It is very important that line managers are the owners and that employees' needs are also considered. Charles Handy (1989) maintains that performance management systems help managers to become 'teachers, counsellors and friends, as much or more than commanders and judges'. He also stresses the collaborative, problem-solving ethos upon which the philosophy is based, as does the Institute of Personnel and Development's position paper (1994):

> employees cannot just be treated as a factor of production... organisations must translate these values into specific and practical action – in too many organisations inconsistency between what is said and what is done undermines trust, generates employee cynicism and provides evidence of contradictions in management thinking.

In other words, performance management is not a way of exploiting employees to get short-term gains in productivity for the employer. People are to be regarded as business partners and there must be a basis of trust, even if it falls short of calling directly for the empowerment of employees. The last part of the quotation above will strike a familiar chord with many NHS managers.

The Contract with Managers

The introduction of performance management, must be seen as a contract made by senior managers with those at departmental level. The chief executive and HR director will be saying to their managers:

> We want to help you achieve a performance-oriented approach – we will provide the organisational systems and framework of support – you create the culture where it can work.

The good professional manager will reply:

> Fine. Just make sure that the system or the way of introducing and running it does not undermine my credibility or control or conflict with the style of management that works for me. It must reflect the values of my staff. Make sure the system is fair and workable and sufficiently well resourced.

The System must Fit

The organisational system must support the manager and should not impose another burden which interferes with patient care, makes demands on time and creates even more paperwork, with little to show for it. Time is important in two ways – the system must be given enough time to be introduced and to settle, and there must be enough time allocated to ensure the process is carried out properly. After all, performance management is likely to involve a considerable change in organisation culture and the existing culture will be resistant to some of its ideas. It also relies on good appraisal and communications.

The Dangers

There is always the danger that senior managers will buy performance management 'packages' that do *not* fit the existing culture. The package will have built into it wrong assumptions about the values and motives of professional staff – perhaps it will require an unwelcome kind of performance measurement component. In looking for standardisation it may be seen as inflexible and insensitive to local differences and needs. Perhaps its introduction will be imposed without creating any sense of ownership at departmental manager level and it will thus be seen as an unwanted alien import. Or there will be mixed messages when tighter staffing levels and higher throughput requirements are imposed without consultation, while managers are being exhorted to improve participation through staff appraisal.

What any performance management system *should* do (and *can* do if well enough designed, and introduced consultatively) is to provide the basis for reinforcing good management practice and for building staff confidence in their own capabilities. If it does this then there will be a resonance effect facilitating change. There should be a sense in which everyone says 'this way of doing things is right for us – we feel we *own* it'.

How will it fit a healthcare environment? To answer this we need to identify the nature of the new management agenda in healthcare in the UK.

The New Management Agenda in Healthcare

Although performance management is new to many healthcare organisations, it fits in with the other radical changes in thinking that have taken place over the last few years.

The reforms to the NHS have led to new thinking about performance. Healthcare is a business which must be competitive and customer-oriented. Administration has given way to general management. Although there are politically contentious issues here, there will be no return to the culture of the past. We need first to look at the wider picture in order to see performance management in context.

What is this New Agenda?

Listed below are the headline changes that have occurred in British healthcare management since 1985. There are widespread rationalisations for all these changes, but they have not all gone down well with every clinical manager. I have recorded the headlines and some of the responses we have seen and will also try to show the links they have with performance management.

Purchasing is Separated from Provision of Services

Having separate organisations dealing with purchasing healthcare for the community and delivery can help clarify objectives and helps create a healthcare market offering competition on quality and price. The contracting process has suddenly become the key to survival.

Performance management certainly has a part to play in developing competitiveness and in offering a means to achieving high quality and productivity.

Healthcare Units become more Autonomous Business Units

Thinking of healthcare as a business in competition with others does not come easy to all clinical staff. In some cases they fear that professional communications and concern for patient welfare will be lost in the rush for business. On the other hand, there are some services that have embraced the market eagerly, all too ready to drive off the opposition from professional colleagues. Mission statements and business plans are now everywhere. The negotiation for resources between the different parts of the organisation is based on business arguments (eg, is it cost-effective? Is there a sound market?) rather than on the old values of precedent or status, or on the basis of an agreed waiting list, for instance. Decisions about intrinsic worth in healthcare terms are left to the purchasers, and business managers and contract negotiators advise clinical directors on how best to respond to the market needs.

Performance management is based on a business model where objectives can be cascaded and responsibilities delegated on the basis of awareness of overall objectives. The processes set up for planning and monitoring of costs and activity can be translated through performance management systems to individual and team targets.

General Management Replaces Administration

Managers now have to set targets and make decisions. General management has sought to allow these decisions to be made as close as possible to the point of service delivery. In the past accountability was through many professional groups each jealously preserving their autonomy, with administrators oiling the wheels of the often intractable and unmanageable healthcare machinery. Where interests differed problems were frequently unresolved. Now there is a single accountability, with professionals reporting to managers who do not necessarily share their training, values and traditions.

Performance management of the right kind might be a vehicle for integration of different interests and commitment to over-arching objectives. Or it might be seen as an alien import.

Resource and Capital Management become a Priority

It gets harder for any clinical professional to maintain a purely clinical role, without being in some sense a manager of resources (and probably having a budget to look after) as well. At the same time, there has been a growth in accountants, business managers, information specialists, non-executive directors, human resource specialists and management consultants, all with ideas on how services could be run better. The return on capital investment was never an issue for clinicians in an organisation where all funding flowed down through bureaucratic tiers. One either learned how to play the bidding and allocation systems or faced frustration, but not extinction of one's service. Deficits were often carried over. Now, there are new demands and heavier penalties for failing. To survive, directorates need to meet financial targets as well as those for service quality, so even first-line clinical managers must understand business priorities and manage budgets.

The organisation must have a means to get service providers to take on business objectives. Is performance management this means?

Restructuring of Organisations, Work and Jobs

The restructuring of organisations in terms of clinical directorates and service centres has encouraged the breaking down of professional boundaries and also significantly reduced career opportunities. As units of management, clinical directorates are small enough to involve people directly in the achievement of targets set in the business plan. Organisations are now 'flatter', ie with fewer tiers of management in service departments. Spans of control of 20 or 30 are common. This means the professional practitioners (say, at ward sister level) now have more management responsibility and fewer senior people to turn to for advice. At the same time there has been a growth in specialist managers, especially in finance and information. Many business and service manager jobs have been merged.

Traditional job roles are no longer sacrosanct. Nurses may take on some of the work previously done only by doctors. New, hybrid, staff with job titles such as *patient associate* and *'care assistant'* are appearing in the wards and clinical departments. National Vocational Qualifications offer the opportunity for people to acquire specific competences on the job, rather than be subjected to the professional educational experience of the past.

To human resource managers it is a more rational way of developing and using scarce and expensive skills. All this challenges traditional assumptions about the necessary qualifications and status. Some professionals have been unhappy about these changes. feeling deskilled, isolated, and excluded from management.

The approach taken to performance management can reinforce positive and negative reactions to change. It should be concerned with developing the right management process in difficult circumstances, that is, amid greater insecurity, with less upward promotion, and with an overwhelming number of busy people to be appraised.

Care Moves to the Community

This has created a more demand-led service. Power has moved from hospital consultants to GPs and community purchasers. This is a less controlled setting, where there is a need to guard against risk not by the bureaucratic controls of the hospital 'bleep culture' but through clear protocols, self-monitoring and high investment in training. The appropriate form of organisation is into small responsive teams who work together flexibly with far more autonomy.

This change in culture requires a delegation of responsibility, extraordinarily good systems for communication and staff support. Development-based performance management fits these requirements well.

Customer Care and Communications are Highlighted

In past eras there was a feeling that professionals were automatically customer-conscious. Yet, however good the service offered clinically, there were obvious failings in the area of basic customer care when compared with commercial organisations. Now in the NHS we have The Patient's Charter – felt by some to be a cosmetic exercise, probably concealing some serious inadequacies. Now patients are being advised what they should expect. As the pressure tightens, stretching meagre resources further and further, there are fears that something will snap. Others have questioned the wisdom of raising customer expectations without increasing resources.

Some new objectives need to be communicated to staff, and appropriate performance measures need to be found.

Flexibility in Staff Pay and Rewards

The NHS has traditionally rewarded time serving rather than high achievement. This has suddenly changed – all NHS Trusts are now obliged to create their own local pay arrangements without much in the kitty for inducement. The old, complex, rigid, nationally-determined system of pay and allowances is crumbling. Traditional career development paths and automatic entitlement to (largely free) professional education no longer exist. Intuitive ideas of quality and competence are being replaced by quantifiable and validated indices.

Many Trusts are considering performance related pay, but there are also possibilities of using other kinds of reward not related directly to remuneration: development opportunities, for instance.

Expansion of Information and Information Systems

A service run on business principles must have the information it needs to plan and monitor its activity levels, its service quality, its use of resources (including human resources), and to generate indexes of performance against targets.

A performance management system must support the information strategy – and vice versa. Staff performance data are vital.

A new, more Vigorous Approach to Service Quality

Purchasers of healthcare are now able to specify quality required in contracts. There must be some process within the organisation to achieve and monitor it. Everyone now takes complaints more seriously, and the customer focus involves consideration of 'shop window' and patient information issues as well as of technical and clinical service quality.

Quality and performance measurement must feature in performance management schemes but managers should appreciate professional sensitivities and their suspicions of involvement by management.

A Clearer Idea of Required Management Competences

Management competence standards for the NHS based on the Management Charter Initiative standards have been developed. Other NVQ competences have been introduced to equip or provide usefully trained care workers.

The clearer identification of training needs and performance standards is helpful and can support performance management and appropriate staff development.

This then, is the managerial character of the new NHS. With it comes a discarding of some aspects of the old management style, now considered outmoded. Gone are the many of the old hierarchies with separately defined accountabilities and with them the assumptions that only certain people can do certain jobs. Separation of professional work from its management no longer applies. Unquestioned clinical autonomy and the belief that clinical work should not be affected by resourcing concerns are things of the past. So are sacrosanct staffing levels and 'jobs for life'. So too is the idea that professionals *can only be* managed by other professionals and that incapable people are retained.

Performance Management and the New Agenda

Choosing the Corporate Strategy

To the NHS tossed on the stormy seas of change, performance management might appear as a vision of the future (if not a life raft for survival in the present). Personnel directors have recognised the part performance management can play in improving performance, which can be seen as part of the business of getting added value from the staff resource, and there are obvious links with other corporate strategies (see Figure. 2.1). It has inevitably become linked with the introduction of local pay policies to replace Whitley Council ones, with performance related pay pencilled into the plans. Anticipating increased productivity, some chief executives will see it as a chance to make quick savings by reducing staffing. However, if long-term added value is to be had from performance management, a more patient and cautious approach will be necessary.

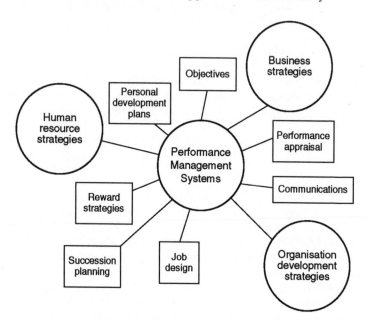

Figure 2.1 Performance management systems and other corporate strategies

Staff may well have a suspicion of management initiatives, based on failure to deliver in the past. Apparently many employees do not believe that the NHS Trusts would be in a position to honour promises of performance related pay, because they believe that the demands for expenditure on patient care would always take precedence. Certainly, there are no benefits (and no trust) without the investments being 'up front'. Many staff identify strongly with their patients. So, despite the pressures on finance, each Trust must consider its investment in people as well as fabric by developing a strategy for investing in and using human resources.

The choice will be between performance management based mainly on pay incentives and performance management based mainly on staff development. The level of investment, the source of it, and the expected return on it will need to be established.

Whatever the combination of factors in the strategic equation, any human resource strategy that does *not* include a strategy for performance management is unlikely to succeed. This is not so much about obtaining short-term gains in productivity as it is about developing a culture where people are more performance-oriented, to provide longer-term benefits to the organisation. The new culture will not however transform deep-rooted views and values overnight, and its introduction must be treated as a major cultural change for the organisation (see Figure 2.2). How might it work out in the NHS?

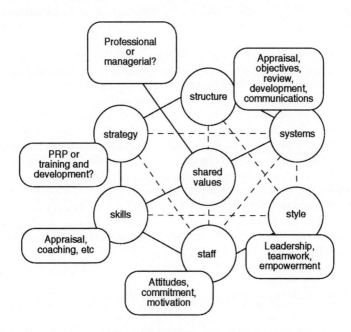

Figure 2.2 Impact of performance management on the organisation (using the systems model developed by McKinsey & Co)

Will Patients and Service Users Benefit?

Many NHS staff feel that the current business orientation is primarily about learning to make do with less, pursuing productivity and efficiency with little return to individual patients. Savings may not be reinvested in patient care. Others may feel that all the time spent in appraisal and the other paraphernalia of performance management systems merely takes up precious time that should be spent in direct care activities. To ensure the right outcomes for patients we need to apply the ultimate criterion of patient benefit to all the activities we undertake. It may be hard to demonstrate how the achievement of any chosen performance objective leads to patient benefit, or whether the performance management scheme in operation is resource-efficient. Yet we should find it easier to reflect on our experience of the wastage and neglect of patient needs that unfocused effort and poor performance inevitably bring.

Traditional Management of Performance and Standards of Practice

Does *new* necessarily mean *better*, though? Healthcare professionals have traditionally had control over the means of setting and maintaining their own standards. They have done this through codes of practice and conduct, self-monitoring of performance (based on published norms and protocols), by accreditation, by job and grade definition, and by nominating supervisors in the workplace to give advice and support. Mentors, coaches and counsellors facilitate professional education which has had a high profile and been relatively accessible to qualified staff. A great deal of appraisal, assessment and development goes on both in and out of the workplace. Professional disciplinary procedures are used to enforce standards and preclude those who fail to meet them. Does this framework provide the basis for adapting to the new performance management requirements?. The answer is 'partly'. The first problem is: whose standards are to be used?

Who Defines Performance Requirements?

We must not assume that professional staff and general managers will agree in their definitions of ideal performance. Managers may put more emphasis on throughput, resource use, and on the more basic customer care standards as defined in The Patient's Charter. Clinical professionals will probably be more concerned with high clinical standards, processes, appropriate competencies and staffing levels. Both will espouse patient welfare as a priority, but may interpret it differently. This is an important question and is likely to determine whether performance management is based on an integrated approach, embracing *everyone's* objectives, or relates only to meeting a *narrow range* of targets set by management and is therefore seen as peripheral to clinical standards. To understand these issues better, we need to explore some underlying values.

Whose Interests and Values does Performance Management Serve?

Clinical professionals (including doctors) will maintain that they want to be adequately rewarded for their skills but are not passively waiting to be enticed by synthetic incentives or management gimmicks to give of their best. They will stress that they practise as individuals and their competence can only be assessed by their professional colleagues. The healthcare outcomes they produce are fairly intangible and are the result of teamwork between professionals. Many would say that managers should be creating the conditions where they can practise effectively rather than attempting to measure their performance and put pressure on them to achieve results that do not coincide with their own values and priorities for care.

On the other hand, some fear that performance management might be used by management to dispense with professional staff and replace them with workers who do not have a vocational approach but who can be better manipulated by extrinsic rewards. That looks like a high-risk strategy which will lead to a battle neither side can win. So there is a need for professionals to influence the process, and for managers to allow that to happen if performance management is to work in healthcare.

Can Managerial and Professional Interests be Integrated?

While some of the traditional professional culture does support the new initiatives, there are some omissions and some contradictions. An integrated approach is prevented if, for example, appraisals are only concerned with professional development and management objectives are neglected – if, for instance, there is a reluctance to set and measure performance standards for non-clinical work. It also depends on preventing too much professional exclusiveness in assessment and learning. Managerial and general competences must feature in professional training.

There are many reasons why clinical professionals should manage services in future, rather than leaving the task to managers without their professional training. Performance management is likely to be part of the management process, and is a tool which can be made to facilitate several kinds of achievement. It can serve the values they hold dear, such as professional autonomy and development, with the rewards coming from achieving high standards of patient care. On the other hand, it can be framed to emphasise short-term gains in productivity, the use of extrinsic rewards, and the elimination of professional control. There is a need, sooner or later, to integrate professional and managerial cultures (and personnel), and to find a *mission statement* that will appeal to all the stakeholders – and makes performance management relevant to issues of clinical practice.

A term such as *'performance orientation'* is unlikely to appeal to health professionals unless it covers a broader range of activities and standards of excellence than those related just to managing organisational resources and meeting Patient's Charter standards. It also needs to embrace the possibility of striving for clinical excellence and ensuring staff development. I would like to use the words *'achievement culture'* rather than performance orientation in order to encompass professional as well as managerial aspirations, and also to remove the connotations of athletic productivity that performance orientation has.

Conditions for Successful Implementation

To succeed, performance management requires open communication. There must be willingness to encourage the participative involvement of all staff, who must for their part be willing to accept the need for change and development. Performance management offers the prospect of a management style based on partnership and can be the means of building a unified organisation. If a system is imposed without consultation and too quickly, the initiative will backfire. In a climate of distrust it will be seen as a manipulative tool. This requires that all parties are seen to have a stake in the outcomes, that they respect each other's values, and have the means of influencing the overall objectives.

We have already mentioned professional standards as a potential source of conflict. The creation of performance incentives may also be. Incentives provided must work in everyone's interest. Rewarding high performers, for instance, is not as simple as it appears. We must check our assumptions about the things that staff perceive as worthwhile for them (and which will motivate them to perform well) or the whole system will fail. Anticipated rewards must be delivered, as promised, in the right amounts and in a timely way without giving *any* staff perceptions of themselves as losers, or the feeling of being manipulated or taken for granted.

Traditionally, occupational groups in healthcare have had very different terms of employment, and therefore had differing expectations. Professional work is organised differently from that of support staff. Different categories of staff will require some variation in the kinds of objectives set. Schemes designed for managers will need modification if they are to be used for non managerial staff. The work of ancillary staff may require setting standards rather than objectives. Some staff will normally work in teams of interdependent people. There are also specialists whose objectives are likely to be unique. How will doctors be incorporated? Different directorates with their own cultures and management styles (such as pathology services or pharmacy) will want the scope to adapt the system to their own culture, which may already have developed some elements independently.

It might be tempting to bring all staff into a standardised performance management system at once. However, there are likely to be important differences between different parts of the organisation which suggests a more cautious, piecemeal approach. If so, the overall aim of integration is in danger of being lost. Yet allowing variations makes it hard to make comparisons (for example in determining entitlement to performance related pay). If ancillary workers have a different scheme from professionals, then teamwork may be put at risk and 'us and them' attitudes will be perpetuated.

Summary

Performance management can refer to *an organisational philosophy*, a management *process* or a set of *formal systems*.

Benefits claimed include: direct improvements in performance and communications and capability; and better use and development of staff. Many organisations have yet to realise these benefits because they have failed to adequately specify values and objectives, or devote sufficient attention to employee communication and consultation or the evaluation of outcomes.

The introduction of performance management should provide the basis for reinforcing good management practice and for building staff confidence in what they can achieve.

Some investments are necessary, particularly in training and in the provision of incentives. For organisations, performance management offers a return on investment but it must be judged as a longer-term strategy rather than a way of achieving better results in the short term at minimal cost. Performance improvement may be based mainly on pay incentives or on staff development.

The system for performance management must support the manager and fit the existing organisational culture. Recently, the more competitive environment for healthcare and structural reorganisations have placed more emphasis on performance. This could lead to conflict with some entrenched traditional values. The form of performance management which emerges must reflect both manager's aims and the values of staff if it is to be effective.

Performance management may come to be concerned with a narrow managerial agenda of efficient use of resources, or alternatively embrace professional standards in a more integrated approach. If the latter is to work in the NHS it needs to take account of what staff find rewarding and motivating, the control desired by professional staff over their work, the kind of measurements of performance employed, and the need to ensure benefit to patients.

Chapter 3

Just What does it Take? How to Maximise Achievement

This chapter looks at the overall process by which staff are motivated for achievement in a health service environment, and examines the factors which can affect it at individual, team and organisational level. This does no real justice to the vast amount of research that has been done into motivation, but is intended to give the reader a framework that is useful when we are thinking about what affects performance. To begin with we need to return to the ideas of expectancy theory, outlined in Chapter 1.

The Performance Equation

The Link between Effort, Performance and Outcome

In Chapter 1 we said that the principle of expectancy theory was that efforts made by individuals depend on their *perception* that these efforts are *likely* to bring about the personal outcomes (rewards) they desire. In other words, for a reward to affect a person's decision to exert effort, people must believe that his or her effort will increase the probability of their obtaining the reward.

So long as the individual believes that, by exerting effort, they can increase the likelihood of their obtaining the reward, then the reward could act as a motivator. For purposes of motivation, it is the *link between effort and reward* that is important. Rewards that come anyway (like a free

Christmas lunch) do not act as motivators. In some cases people are motivated even though success is not certain, provided they feel they have some chance (for instance, working in competition with others to win a prize). If they felt that success was impossible, they would not be motivated.

When a reward is given, it is usually for the *results* of the effort rather than for the effort itself. One rarely rewards effort unless the effort has resulted in a good performance, eg, increased output, or better quality. Here it is the *performance* which is being rewarded.

Low effort and poor performance could result in punishment or a withholding of reward. We can build this into our model simply by using the word 'outcome' (ie, outcome for the individual) rather than 'reward'. Outcomes can be either positive or negative.

In this book, to prevent confusion with other meanings of the term, we shall refer to these motivational outcomes simply as rewards (we could also use the word reinforcements). This model of motivation is depicted in Figure 3.1.

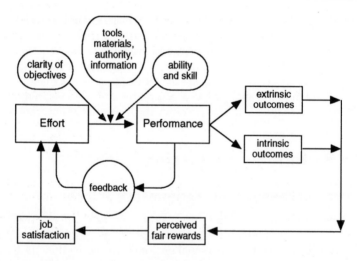

Figure 3.1 Factors affecting motivation (expectancy theory)

Linking Effort and Performance

Effort and performance are not synonymous. We all know individuals whose efforts are great but whose performance is in some way poor. There may be a number of reasons for this, related to both individual attributes and the working environment. There must be a strong positive correlation between effort and performance if the personal outcomes provided are to motivate the individual.

What can prevent a person's efforts from resulting in good performance?

Lack of Direction and Focus
'I didn't know *what* you wanted'. Many bosses do not make clear to their subordinates just what it is that they require, or check that the subordinate has understood and feels able to meet the requirements.

'*I didn't know **how** to do it*' : Even if the required results are apparent, the means of achieving them may not be, so procedures always need to be clear.

Lack of Competence
There are a number of sensitive issues here. The person may simply lack the necessary skills or knowledge to be successful in the task. Where lack of ability or know-how is impairing performance, some kind of diagnosis of the learning need is essential. This might indicate that to be effective the individual needs to acquire a basic skill, to learn to make discriminations, to memorise information or to anticipate effects, for example. Failing to recognise and use existing skills can damage motivation.

Resources
Lack of resources has a double effect – it not only hampers performance directly, it also affects motivation. The employee sees poor performance as due to factors outside his or her control. When asked to list resources people readily mention tools, materials and equipment, and money. However time and manpower are often in very short supply. One resource which people often neglect is information. Yet all care staff will be aware of the frustration that occurs when progress comes to a halt because some vital piece of patient information is missing. Once information systems are working well, people realise that setting priorities, and planning the use of time, manpower and other resources becomes much easier.

Task Integration
The design of the task often influences the link between effort and performance. Some jobs give individuals little control over their work. Professional staff sometimes complain that their contact with the patient is fragmentary. Multidisciplinary case conferences enable a more coordinated approach and enable the efforts of team members to become focused towards a common purpose. Technicians who are trained to carry out a series of linked tasks are better able to turn their efforts into effective

performance. The design of the overall work system or environment can also hamper work performance. There may be duplication of effort, or people get in each other's way, or there are gaps in communication, for example.

Capacity and Overload

It may be that the individual is being expected to do more than he or she can really cope with. Performance is impaired by conflicts of tasks and priorities. While it is proven that a certain amount of pressure within limits, enhances performance, there is clear evidence that pushing people beyond those limits impairs performance and results in stress. More recently it has been discovered that some people do learn to work on 'overdrive' for fixed periods, but the long-term results appear to lead to errors of judgements and more serious breakdown.

The overloading of organisational systems is common in the NHS. Greater output is expected than the input resources (eg, equipment and materials) allow. This is like operating a machine without adequate servicing.

A weak link between effort and performance may be because the efforts are used inefficiently as when someone lacks the ability to achieve skilled performance. However, just as important is the psychological link where effort is not felt by the employee to be producing results. A lot depends on what the person *believes* about the situation.

Blocks and Barriers

In traditional organisations, much depends on the local organisational culture -'how we do things round here'. This culture can give out signals that become powerful disincentives and *social and cultural barriers*. Barriers to high performance and innovation can be caused by rigid bureaucratic practices. People's capacity to perform at their best is often diminished by lack of status or authority. So-called 'glass ceilings' can prevent people, typically women or disabled people, from progressing beyond a prescribed level of seniority or responsibility. One comment when clinical directors were being appointed from the ranks of medical consultants was 'the glass ceiling has now become double glazed!' We can identify many similar examples.

The Performance–Reward Link

The level of motivation is also affected by the links between individual performance and the expected outcomes for the individual. If a person believes he or she is performing well, but this does not result in reward, then effort may dry up. Similarly if there is no unfavourable personal outcome (eg, punishment) resulting from recognised poor performance either, then there may be no particular reason to improve.

The Reward Itself

Intrinsic and Extrinsic Rewards

The achievement of a desired result is in itself often rewarding for an individual who believes their efforts and performance have brought it about. We can refer to such rewards as *intrinsic*, to distinguish them from *extrinsic* rewards. *Intrinsic* rewards *are inherent in doing the job*, for instance contributing to patient recovery, appreciation, satisfaction – from using one's skills or solving different problems. *Extrinsic* rewards are applied from *outside the situation*, according to some assessment of results, like a bonus or commission, for instance. They also include social and non-material things such as recognition of achievement by others, status and prestige, as well as a raft of applied incentives such as bonuses and increments based on performance. There is a great deal of evidence that intrinsic rewards are very important for most healthcare workers. That does not mean that money and other extrinsic rewards can be neglected, but that there may be problems in assuming that clinical care standards and productivity can be manipulated by cash rewards.

Expectancy theory does not tell us what rewards will be most effective in providing motivation over what timescale. It does however suggest some essential requirements for rewards to work:

- *Immediacy of rewards* – the immediacy of the rewards may be very significant. The more senior the job, the more likely it is that the knowledge of any reward being offered will be delayed. It may be a long time before the results of performance are known, and the extrinsic reward (eg, performance related pay) is often allocated on an annual basis.
- *Value of rewards* – rewards offered must be valued strongly enough to influence behaviour. We shall see in Chapter 11 that this is a problem in the application of performance pay to the NHS, where people like to put caring for the patient high on their list of satisfactions, and where the availability of resources to fund performance pay at levels high enough to be effective is in doubt.
- *Withholding of reward* – withholding a reward is likely to be ineffective in generating high levels of performance. The person will do just enough to avoid the deprivation, but no more. Punishment can lead to passive behaviour and resentment.
- *Praise and censure* – quite often individuals complain about being taken for granted. Sometimes there is a lack of recognition of who has been

responsible, and at other times thanks are not passed on. Sometimes people find it hard to reprimand staff and they continues to be unaware that their behaviour or performance is unsatisfactory. It is damaging if anticipated rewards which do not materialise.

'I did the extra shift so that I could have Thursday off, but they couldn't spare me.'
'We were told that too many staff had an above average grading so they couldn't afford to pay the level of performance pay that we had been promised.'
'We have been making do with our completely inadequate equipment because we were promised new equipment – now you tell us it's been cancelled because of overspends elsewhere.'

Here are some further conditions for the use of rewards (personal outcomes) to be effective in persuading people to make the effort to improve performance:

- Employees must believe that improved performance will be rewarded.
- Targets must be ones which people can be motivated to work for.
- Performance must be measurable and clearly attributed to the individual or team.
- The means and results of assessment must be fair to individuals and groups.
- Achievement of rewards must not conflict with other values and priorities.

Communication Requirements

The Importance of Feedback

If a reward is to have any effect on a person's behaviour the person must have information about performance, results obtained and the delivery of rewards which result. For example:

'Is the effort I am making leading to the desired performance?'
'Is my performance getting results (and the rewards that I value)?'

If the answer is 'no', then the worker may give up. But if the answer is 'I don't know', then the individual is not much better off.

The essential knowledge of results to guide people's actions is not always available in healthcare. Sometimes a patient is discharged or passed on to someone else before staff know whether their efforts have been of use, or appreciated by the patient or other care staff. Even more difficult is getting data on the longer term impact of what is done. It may be some time before it filters back to us that something was not done quite as required, or quickly enough, or with the right information. The manager who says nothing when things are satisfactory, but comes down like the proverbial ton of bricks when things go wrong, is legendary.

Avoiding these mistakes means identifying expectations to begin with, comparing the results with expectation, and making it easy for people to seek, get and use the feedback they need. This takes courage, sensitivity and planning on the manager's part. Appraisal and performance review meetings provide a crucial exchange of this kind of information, but good quality feedback must be available all the time.

We need communication processes that transmit appropriate information to guide appropriate behaviour, increase motivation, and enable people to learn. People need information about what is required of them, whether rewards are being provided, and actual performance. The information must flow in each direction, at the right time. The appraisal process has a major part to play here, in both its formal and informal forms.

Here are some everyday examples illustrating communication failures that affect effort–performance–reward links:

What expectations are there about *effort* required?
'I wish you'd tried a bit harder with Dr Fletcher, his cooperation is vital.'

Does *effort* lead to *the right level of performance*?
'I know you spent hours on this procedure, but we had to do it again the next day.'

Does good performance lead to the required results?
'If the team had seen what I had recommended, then the patient would be back home by now.'

Were the results reported back to the person involved – for their learning?
'I still don't know whether all that work I put in was worthwhile.'

Is the effort and performance *recognised*?
'Nobody said thank you.'

So, if we wish to improve performance at work, we need to consider five distinct factors:

- the effort–performance relationship
- the performance–reward relationship
- the type of reward
- the feedback of information to the individual
- barriers hindering performance and communication.

The above separation of factors is in fact quite useful when we want to analyse what is going wrong with performance in a given situation.

Other Motivation Theories

I hope I have established the usefulness of the expectancy theory model. Its limitations seem to be that it says nothing about the relative power of different personal outcomes or rewards. It is hard to apply to the motivation of teams. We now turn to other theories of motivation to expand the picture we have of what motivates people.

Needs-based theories

Some well known theories of motivation assume that rewards (*or reinforcements*) change behaviour because in so doing the individual can satisfy some underlying *need*. Most readers will be familiar with the theories of Maslow (1970). He suggested that people's needs operate in an ascending hierarchy. Once basic physiological needs like food and shelter are satisfied we seek security, then belonging, then esteem, then self-actualisation.

Alderfer simplified this by talking about existence needs (basic survival), relatedness needs and personal growth needs (see Handy, 1993). He suggested that we could seek to satisfy more than one need at once but that if people's higher-level needs were thwarted, they would put more effort into meeting the lower-level needs. Hence if job satisfaction is unattainable, people will concentrate on improving their social relationships or press for more pay.

Herzberg (1966) said that needs were of two sorts: hygiene factors and motivating factors. Hygiene factors (poor conditions, bad supervision, difficult relationships, etc) do not motivate and cannot be a source of satisfaction. They simply act to demotivate and are a source of dissatisfaction, when neglected. So-called 'motivators' create satisfaction. People will work for these indefinitely. They include opportunity for achievement and influence, recognition, responsibility and advancement, often work itself.

On the other hand, some people will be prepared to work hard for low immediate needs satisfaction, where work is scarce, or where people are beginning a career and believe that satisfaction will occur later on. At other times, attempting to meet needs at work will have little effect, for example, a member of staff whose needs for recognition and affiliation are already met outside the organisation in family and social activities.

Although these theories may be of value in seeing how motivation works, people work for different goals, create their own perceptions of reality and interpret the same facts in different ways. People's *perception* of situations, particularly of what seems *fair*, seem to influence people's behaviour a great deal in practice. Expectancy theory enables us to build such perceptions into a model of the motivational process.

The Psychological Contract
Handy (1993) points out that motivation has come to mean 'getting other people to want what you want them to want'. Applying mechanistic theories can be degrading if it leads to a manipulative style of management. A more useful idea is that of the 'psychological contract' (Schein, 1965), which refers to what an individual expects from the organisation in return for what it expects from him or her. According to Handy, 'motivation' happens when the contract is balanced. This idea is particularly useful in the context of appraisal and objective setting, because it recognises the two-way nature of the relationship, and conveys a sense of partnership which can lead easily to the idea of an explicit performance agreement with which both parties are happy, rather than seeing it as a question of manipulation of workers by managers.

Effort is Influenced by the Setting of Goals

In some studies it was found that setting explicit goals was an important mediating factor on performance. Provided people accepted the setting of goals as reasonable, the higher the goal, the better people performed. It is the setting of goals that has a major influence on the effort expended, not the perception of the likelihood of reward. Rewards are needed to *maintain* the goal behaviour, or may be used to induce people to change their goals. This will depend on people accepting the legitimacy of the goals being set.

Motivation of the 'Dedicated Professional'

Professional healthcare workers' motivation is different from many other groups. They are likely to be committed to working to achieve personal outcomes such as a level of patient care which provides satisfaction for them, or the recognition of professional excellence. It appears that they will work harder and harder to achieve difficult goals which support these outcomes. For many skilled technical and care workers there is an intrinsic interest in their work which means they are often willing to put in long hours to solve challenging problems.

Imposing incompatible goals, perhaps based on productivity rather than care standards, for extrinsic rewards such as money, is unlikely to induce them to change their behaviour. They may even prefer not to practise at all and leave the profession, if they are not able to work in the way they want to. There is a traditional sense of being part of a service requiring dedication to duty, and some get evident satisfaction from identifying with the status of the uniform.

Job Design and Empowerment

There is evidence that if certain features are present in jobs, staff will achieve satisfaction and be motivated to perform. The job should:

- form some identifiable integrated task or objective
- be seen by the job-holder as meaningful and worth doing
- allow for decisions to be made by the job-holder
- give direct feedback on effectiveness
- provide fair rewards for the efforts made.

This fits in well with expectancy theory and helps maximise the motivators that Herzberg identifies. The advent of primary nursing could be seen as improving the job of registered nurses. Recently there has been an interest in empowerment as a means of ensuring that staff are given maximum control over what they are doing, are free to pursue innovative solutions and are encouraged to engage as closely as possible with customers. In most healthcare contexts this will call for high levels of trust, competence, delegation and acceptance of responsibility and teamwork. Innovation must be balanced against risk.

We can now provide a checklist that can be used to spot the cause of any performance deficiency.

Requirements for Performance to be Effective

- Are direction and goals clear and achievable but stretching?
- Does the person have the required competence – ie, adequate skills or knowledge?
- Is resourcing adequate? (Consider finance, staffing, time, information, materials or equipment.)
- Does the person have appropriate authority and status?
- Are we sure individuals and system are not overloaded?
- Are there bureaucratic or cultural barriers to success?

- Are the rewards (personal outcomes) that are provided both valued and sufficient?
- Is there the right balance between the individual's and organisation's expectations?
- How effective is feedback (eg, for knowledge of results, performance appraisal)?
- Does the design of jobs offer post-holders control and integration?
- Is there scope for initiative and empowerment?

Of course this might be seen as simplistic, as there are complex interactions between these factors, and people are far from predictable. It does, however, provide us with a model for performance management.

Summary

Expectancy theory provides a useful model of how effort, performance and rewards are related. It suggests that to achieve effective motivation we need to consider:

the effort-performance relationship
the performance-personal outcomes relationship
the personal outcomes available
the feedback of information to the individual
barriers hindering performance and communication.

We must take account of the needs of the individual if we are to provide personal outcomes that people will want to work for. There is evidence that these operate as a hierarchy and that once more basic needs are satisfied, people seek satisfaction of social and achievement needs. We can distinguish between personal outcomes that *de*motivate if *not* present (like adequate working conditions) but which do not themselves motivate, and personal outcomes that *directly* motivate (like recognition).

There is also evidence that the setting of explicit goals which call for high performance are effective in achieving results. It is essential to take account of the differing perceptions and expectations of the individual in terms of the psychological contract, and motivation is more likely to occur when there is a balanced relationship between the employee and the organisation, which is felt to be fair one. Empowerment is a means of harnessing employee commitment by allowing scope for problem solving and creativity. Figure 3.2 builds on our model in Figure 3.1 to include many of these elements.

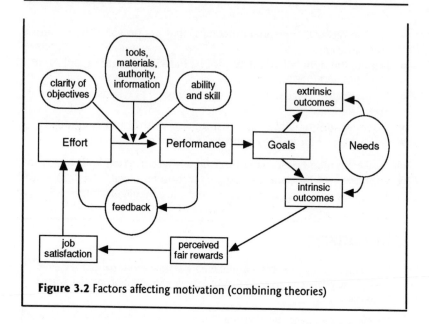

Figure 3.2 Factors affecting motivation (combining theories)

Chapter 4

Prescription for Achievement: How to Manage for Results

Some important components for a management style that leads to high performance and achievement are highlighted in this chapter. The case studies introduce examples and are followed by some characteristics which research and experience have shown to be important.

The Impact of Management Style

Consider the two management styles described below. In each case decide whether the manager is effective in maximising the performance of the staff she supervises and also the likely response of staff to the management style described.

Manager A

Joan works with a clear set of procedures. Over a long period of time she has developed systems and procedures that work. She has high standards and prides herself that all her staff are trained to those standards. Anybody wanting to change things has to refer to her. She carries out regular inspections of the whole department to ensure that everything is being done properly. Her meetings with staff are to explain changes in procedure, and there is a good deal of complaint from everybody about management.

She prides herself on running a tight ship, where everybody has a clear brief and standards are clear, enforced by disciplinary action if necessary. 'I take ultimate responsibility for everything that happens here. Anyone with a complaint must see me. You can always bleep me if there is a problem.' Staff development means nothing more than instructing people in new procedures and techniques. Staff sometimes feel left in the dark about changes that are imposed.

Manager B

Amanda believes in delegation. She encourages her staff to find their own solutions to problems. 'I want people to feel empowered' she says, 'to take responsibility for themselves, not be treated like children.' When people ask for instructions, she tends to throw the problem back to them; 'In that way people learn'.

Some problems have arisen recently, however. She had delegated the drawing-up of rosters to a fairly junior person in the department, and there were a lot of complaints that these were not satisfactory. There was also a dispute between some of the senior staff over who had overall responsibility for admissions. Some of the more menial tasks were being neglected. The meeting called to discuss these problems had not resolved them. Amanda had told them that they must work as a team, and she did not want people to become possessive and inflexible in their attitudes.

She does not carry a bleep at home. Staff development plans are ambitious, but frequently do not happen. This is a cause of frustration for some people. Change plans are based on democratic discussion but happen rather chaotically.

Both management styles described do have positive features. In the first there is a clear definition of requirements and standards. Accountability is clear. But the manager holds too tightly on to the reins and as a result stifles initiative and development. In the second, the manager wants to develop people and encourage achievement but in so doing allows standards and procedures to be neglected and accountability to become fudged. You can imagine that each produces a different kind of frustration for staff. In the first example people might err on the side of caution, or not take the action required because they did not have the necessary authority. In the second there may be dangers of neglect or in people taking on more than they could cope with. In both cases people feel insufficiently supported in their work. You might also feel that both departments would have some difficulty in achieving change, for different reasons. In the first there is an in-built resistance to any change; in the second there is likely to be a lack of focus, and people will be pursuing uncoordinated objectives, with little monitoring. So in each of these situations it is unlikely that people are going to reach their full potential, or adapt to changing requirements, or even that the department is going to be as productive as it might be.

If we want to develop the potential both for high performance and job satisfaction, we must ensure clear accountability, develop two-way communication and plan the development of staff. Also important are clear targets, feedback and encouragement.

Activity

Are you already a convert to performance management?

If you already manage people, or aspire to do so, check whether you are already in tune with achievement culture ideas by answering the questions below.

1. Everyone in my department knows what our objectives are. YES NO

2. I have standards for individual performance. YES NO

3. If staff come up with good ideas they are often given the chance to implement them. YES NO

4. I hold regular team meetings to discuss progress and improvements and get people's views. YES NO

5. Everyone has an appraisal at least once every three months. YES NO

6. Staff records include a development plan. YES NO

7. People always know when their efforts are appreciated. YES NO

8. People are never in any doubt when they have not met the standards required. YES NO

9. New staff are given a detailed induction to the department. YES NO

10. I use non-financial incentives to encourage good performance. YES NO

11. Staff are frequently asked to teach others what they know. YES NO

These questions give the flavour of performance management at one level. If you answered 'yes' to more than six of these questions it is likely that you already subscribe to some extent to the philosophy of achievement culture – if you had nine or more 'yeses' you are practising it.

In the remainder of this chapter I look in more detail at some of the requirements for a management style that supports achievement.

The Prescription

- Realities
- Priorities
- Time management
- Job clarity and empowerment
- Clear objectives
- Information
- Accountability
- Measurement
- Empowerment
- Communication and teamwork
- Concern for quality
- Promoting change
- Staff development.

Realism

Know what you want to do, and what *can* be done. That is, be clear about priorities, resources and available options.

Priorities

The National Health Service is notoriously bad at setting priorities. In 1993 someone counted over 200 'priorities' that had been mentioned in official circulars. The *Health of the Nation* document was intended to provide a common set of long-term goals. In practice, however, events with political significance ranging from the snatching of babies from maternity units to the advent of so called 'flesh eating killer viruses' has automatically led to calls for additional priorities. Healthcare staff have learned to live with long, changing lists of priorities which are complex and reactive. Organisational priorities may involve achievement of annual business plan objectives; achievement of longer-term objectives and projects; maintaining standards (of care, safety, access etc); keeping within set boundaries or constraints, or avoidance of crisis situations.

In order to make priorities clear to others, the manager's own must be clear. When as a manager you discuss priorities with your own manager, or set priorities with your staff, the following considerations have to be in the manager's mind.

1. The Impact of Overall Organisational Priorities

The effect may be direct or indirect. Priorities for which managers do not have responsibility can affect their work by creaming off available resources or taking their boss's time, for instance. Or there may be a change of direction planned for the organisation that will have implications: for example, changes in market strategy, budgeting or staff terms and conditions.

2. Things for which you will have a Particular Responsibility

It is important to identify the kind of priority, eg, is it 'at all costs we must avoid this' or, 'this must happen (at some time)' or, 'this must happen (straight away!)'? Priorities should be subject to influence but are unlikely to be *too* negotiable or they would probably not be called priorities.

3. Things Important to the Manager Personally

These include things like sorting out the filing system, or ensuring cover for maternity leave, or finding the money to send three staff on an update course. There will be improvements to be made, things to be sorted out, and even personal goals for which managers must find time and resources.

4. Resources Available

Finance, manpower, time, equipment and space are important. So is information. There is some scope for negotiation here. If a priority is set, consider and discuss where resources may need to be *reallocated* to meet new priorities. If the equipment is new, consider the training needs, time required to achieve proficiency and the maintenance requirements.

5. The Manager's Capacity and that of the System

As a manager you must be aware of time constraints, quality standards expected, the authority needed, general workload pressure, system capacity and any plans that have already been agreed. You may be expected to cope with some short-term pressures, but do not allow yourself or your staff to be indefinitely overloaded. Be prepared to consider alternatives and options in solving problems prior to making decisions and recommendations – this may require some thinking or consultation time. Contingency planning may be necessary.

6. Any Limits to Delegation

Sometimes there is a difficulty in delegation, either because of qualification or because of some expectation that one individual will be seen to carry out the task personally (see page 96). The process of prioritising lends itself to objective setting – we shall say more about these issues in Chapters 7 and 8.

The manager receives priorities and transmits priorities to others. Only if you obtain clear priorities from your own senior manager will you be able to convey a clear sense of priorities to staff who report to you. Their needs and concerns when they discuss priorities with you should match yours – so anticipate their questions.

7. Staff Capability, Competence and Capacity

The capability of staff, their experience and training needs must be considered when you are deciding what can reasonably be taken on, and what time limits are being provided for completion. Also important is the capacity of staff. Useful workers are often overloaded.

Managers need to feel confident that they are operating within a realistic framework of what is achievable with the total resource available. Trying to achieve too many priorities will put them all at risk – or lead to staff burnout, or an overload on resources. or a neglect of important day-to-day work. Prudent managers will look to agree fall-back plans as far as possible, but in the current climate there will be no copper-bottomed certainties. In an era where management is assumed to be ascendant, it is surprising how disillusioned many healthcare managers are about the management process in their organisation. You need to be able to cope with setbacks without reverting to crisis management. You will also need to warn staff of the threats to the overall programme and to be able to maintain enthusiasm and commitment when things are not going as planned.

Activity

Can you list all the priorities that you need to attend to?

In each case differentiate between urgency and importance (high, medium, low). Then rank them for urgency and importance. Try to identify the *time commitment* likely to be required for each. Try to identify the non-staff resource required for each. Ask yourself which of them could be delegated? Which can be done only by you? How much staff time will each call for?

Then go on to next stage.

Identify your main priorities. List your queries about priorities and resourcing. Identify things that realistically will not be possible.
Identify things that might conflict, or where careful planning is needed.
Discuss your lists with your boss, and then with your senior staff.

Time Management

It is worth analysing your use of time to identify time-wasters. The highly structured nature of healthcare work, the need to respond to emergencies, the expectations of doctors, all lead to a sense of loss of control over time.

It is important that the manager does not allow all his or her time to be used reactively.

Job Clarity and Empowerment

Explicit Job Roles

High performance depends on people doing the right things. Is absolute clarity always necessary? Might it be better to leave things more vague, to avoid people working too rigidly to job descriptions? There are good reasons for being clear about roles, accountability and authority. If the manager does not attend to these issues a number of problems arise. People will feel confused and unsure about what they can and can't do. Others will assume inappropriate authority. Duplication will occur, often leading to personal conflict and stress. Lines of communication inside and outside the department get muddled. Some vacuums will occur where no one wants to assume responsibility. Time will be wasted reaching consensus where ideas and priorities differ.

Identifying the Right Skill Mix

The *mix* of roles within the department needs to match the demands the manager faces. The mix of Indians and chiefs must be kept under review. It can be wasteful, demoralising and stressful to work with the wrong mix. Many detailed studies of tasks being undertaken have been carried out through work activity sampling. A typical series of studies showed that qualified staff were undertaking many duties that could be done by unqualified staff – there was scope for greater use in clinical areas of clerical staff and trained care assistants. Traditional staffing patterns could often be improved when workload variations are considered. Interestingly, the amount of time staff at a given grade spend on direct patient care varied considerably, even in very comparable situations. It was also found that the amount of waiting time seen to be required can also vary.

A basic requirement then is to ensure that staff capacity is not being wasted or applied to the wrong ends. Skill mix studies sometimes arouse suspicion if the expectation is that outsiders are coming in to demonstrate overstaffing and to recommend cuts. However, if done with an awareness of patient care needs and in collaboration with local managers, such studies can lead to improvements which will enhance both performance and staff morale.

Clear Objectives

Once you have revised and agreed the job roles, you still need to ensure that people are clear about required goals and outcomes, how to go about achieving them, the resources that are available, and the time by which they are needed. All very simple. Or is it? In practice a number of problems can get in the way. Senior management do not appear to know what they want. As a manager you have reservations about the goals set or resources available. The goal posts are moved. The resources dry up. Staff have different ideas on what the goals should be. There may be doubts about people's capability.

In the often chaotic world of the NHS these are common problems. Managers who fail to make their capacity clear may end up having to implement objectives that they are very unhappy about and uncommitted to in order to keep their jobs. This is a recipe for failure. It is important that managers are able to support what they have to implement. It is *not* a good manager who says, 'This is what they want – I don't at all agree with it myself, but we've got to do it' or, 'There's not much chance of achieving this but I had to make the commitment.'

Information

Never underestimate the value of good quality information on performance and activities and resources. Without it, much planning is wasted.

Accountability

By *accountability* we mean answerability to someone for the achievement of particular results. Robert Crosby (1992) has described the conditions for workable accountability as those where people have the authority to do what they are expected to do, with one person accountable for each task. Even on a matrix group across departments, he recommends what he calls 'single point accountability'. People take responsibility for decisions whatever the outcome, and even when this requires seeking the views of others and getting their cooperation.

This is in contrast to consensus decision making with no clear accountability, which Crosby says is time-consuming and is often controlled by the most rigid or resistant members. But this is not a recipe for autocratic management. Indeed, much is lost (in terms of the product and motivation) if influence is not permitted, eg, in suggesting solutions to problems, seeing them acted on, and getting feedback when suggestions are rejected. However, influencing must not be confused with deciding and it must always be clear who has responsibility for getting something done.

Measurement

Identify Input, Throughput and Output Requirements

Model the requirements for your own department as a system. Performance management requires us to think in terms of the inputs, outputs and
processes which make up any operation – in other words in terms of
systems. A systems model helps in a number of ways. It shows important
links and throughputs (eg, patients, forms); it suggests how things relate
and interact (eg, demand/responses); it assists in identifying useful measures (eg, input and output); it helps us predict the effects of particular
changes and interventions. (eg, by using force field analysis); it provides
a visual means of communicating what whole processes are about (eg, to
explain admission or discharge options). See Figure 4.1 and Table 4.1 for
examples. To model performance we need to identify:

- planned outcomes
- input, output and throughput requirements
- output standards
- standards of competence.

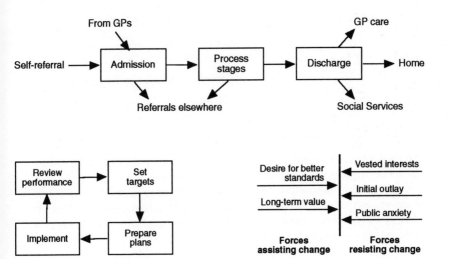

Figure 4.1 Examples of systems models

Table 4.1 *Example results and measures*

Type of planned result	Example measure
patient activity	finished consultant episodes, admissions; patient numbers
efficiency in resource use	units of resource used per case or per volume; saving
cost effectiveness	cost per case; relative cost; saving
speed	time to be seen; time per result; variation from target time
simplicity/complexity	number of stages; number of handlers
breadth of coverage	population categories reached; distribution % covered
precision	deviation; hit rate on target; false positives, etc
responsiveness	time taken; diagnostic accuracy; target criteria; dependency
accessibility	increase in usage
equity	relative outcomes for different categories
clinical standards	target criteria achieved; expressed satisfaction (survey)

Outcomes are not the same as *outputs*. Outcomes are the results or consequences of undertaking an activity – they may be planned or unplanned. Output is the measurable *product* from a process or activity. We can measure output quantitatively. We often use output measures to detect if outcomes have occurred – but many outcomes may not be measurable in this way.

Example: A student takes a course of study. *Input* is 35 hours of tuition and 70 hours of private study. *Output* is three written assignments of 2,000 words and an examination answer of 3,500 words. The *outcomes* were that the student was awarded a pass with distinction and was recommended to take a higher course of study next year.

Empowerment

Staff are empowered by

- Knowing what is required of them.
- Being given the authority and resources to carry it out.
- Taking responsibility for the whole process, not just parts of it.
- Being consulted and having their contribution taken on board.
- Knowing that their contribution is valued and will be rewarded.
- Being trained and developed.
- Having their needs recognised.
- Being trusted, and supported where necessary.
- Working in an atmosphere of problem solving rather than blame.
- Being allowed to take risks even if sometimes failing.
- Being set difficult assignments which they achieve.

Professional staff have strong expectations to be empowered. The absence of the above factors is often disempowering. In a sense this book is all about empowerment.

Create an Atmosphere of Problem Solving rather than of Blame

The resolution of problems is often not helped by attributing blame, or labelling individuals with our adverse judgements. Judgements are often necessary, but we must learn to distinguish judgements from factual statements if we are to create a culture of achievement. Much of the failure in performance appraisal and report writing comes from an inability to make this distinction.

Deliver what was Promised

Sometimes you hear comments like:

'That manager's all talk. She said I could go on that course but I never heard anything more. She said she'd get the steriliser fixed, but we've been waiting a year now. I'm supposed to have an appraisal meeting this week, but I expect it'll be cancelled. She wanted a report from me too; I haven't done it, but she won't complain if it's late.'

There are sometimes very good reasons why deadlines are missed and events postponed, but it does not suggest a culture where achievement is expected. Every deadline missed or ignored is destroying your credibility as a manager who is interested in achievement. It also undermines your own performance and that of your staff.

Are the limits of your own authority and accountability clear?
When delegating, do you consider the authority required?
How is this communicated to others?
Do you stand up for your staff if their authority is challenged?
Is accountability within your teams clearly identified?
Are there situations where you are making the whole team responsible for something (with the result that *nobody* is taking it on board?)
Is professional and managerial accountability sufficiently distinct?
How do you usually indicate to people that their contribution is valued?
In event of failure, does problem solving or blame occur?
Have you allowed people to take risks, even if sometimes they fail?
Are staff set difficult assignments which they go on to achieve?
Have you made promises to staff that you still have to deliver on?
How many staff suggestions have been taken on board recently?
Think about the evidence to support your answers to the above questions.

Communication and Teamwork

High achievement depends on excellent communication and teamwork.

The right communication style to support achievement is one that is *open, informative* and *responsive*.

Open Communication

Open communication requires that information is transmitted fully and without distortion. Disagreements will be viewed as opportunities for dialogue and problem solving. Suggestions for improvements will be encouraged. When there is a need to restrict information or observe confidentiality, the reasons will be understood. Managers should say, 'It is likely that...' or, 'To the best of my knowledge...' when appropriate. This destroys the common belief that managers hold back information.

Informative Communication

This requires making information available and sharing it as much as possible – setting up two-way channels for communication. Efforts must be made to ensure everyone is fully briefed; questions raised have to be answered. Individual expertise is used and willingly shared and background material is made available.

Responsive Communication

This requires needs and requests to be responded to quickly. People will need to make their knowledge available to others. Any need for confidentiality needs to be understood and honoured. Specific appreciation is given for work well done. Problems are identified and dealt with without attribution of blame.

Participation

The manager needs to develop a culture where people are able to influence the way things are done and will take responsibility for change. This can be done by encouraging ideas for improvements and agreeing who will implement them. Managers can build confidence by supporting staff decisions and actions and being open to constructive criticism and suggestions as well as refraining from public criticism of individuals. In other words, to be aware of people's skills and enthusiasms and use and encourage them.

Developing teamwork

Teams are becoming more important in healthcare as the focus moves towards responses to local demand and away from centralised command structures. There are also advantages in working in *effective* teams since a team can achieve more than the sum total of the contributions of the same individuals. A manager can influence those things that facilitate teamwork in interactive teams, where achievement is based on working together:

- ensuring balanced roles within the group
- setting clear objectives and accountability based on agreed goals
- encouraging openness
- ensuring conflicts are identified and dealt with
- developing mutual support and trust
- providing opportunities for cooperation and social interaction
- having sound operating procedures
- providing appropriate leadership
- instituting regular reviews of processes and outcomes
- assisting individual development to take place
- working to create sound inter-group relations
- ensuring effective communications.

Research suggests that participative leadership usually works best except when situations are complex or very demanding, when team members may be happy to see it replaced by a more directive style.

Concern for quality

The manager should work on quality awareness and professional excellence, emphasising quality aspects in all the work carried out. This means that people get used to setting and meeting standards and looking for ways to improve quality without being prompted to do so. Some organisations adopt total quality management or quality circles as part of a performance management strategy. Below are some ideas which may help develop quality awareness on an everyday basis:

- run meetings to agree quality requirements
- ask staff to devise measurement of current quality
- use brainstorming and problem- solving groups to tackle deficiencies
- develop customer surveys (*internal* customers as well as patients and relatives)
- commission projects and objectives that are specifically aimed at improving quality
- undertake studies and comparisons with other departments
- get professional interest groups to undertake action research
- link service quality development to individual staff development programmes – ensure achievements are in professional portfolios
- have presentations by staff (and outsiders) on quality themes
- ensure quality is referred to in all objectives set
- enter competitions and demonstrations
- publicise your achievements and generate high expectations of your team
- develop benchmarks of best practice standards and apply them.

Quality needs to be seen in terms of professional *and* administrative excellence, in terms of clinical *and* non-clinical standards. It is helpful to talk about maximising quality within existing resources. The manager should bear in mind that sometimes staff feel that their conditions of work or equipment are so appalling, or they feel so overloaded, that these needs have to be addressed before quality becomes meaningful or worth pursuing.

Promoting Change

Innovation

Tom Peters (1988) says that the most useful question to ask at appraisal is, 'What exactly have you changed today?' followed by, 'Are you sure? What's next? Exactly what bold goal does the change support?' Survival demands that the rate of learning must be at least as great as the rate of change – so there is clearly a constant need to stimulate creativity and innovation. Some say it is the manager's prime task to strive for continuing change, and to get staff used to change as a way of life.

However, healthcare has been hit by such whirlwinds of change in the past 15 years that many now feel it is time for some consolidation, and building of structures that will last.

There is some cynicism about changes that required enormous effort and commitment but which did not deliver. The position of the manager is paradoxical: providing stability for those who are perplexed and stressed by the pace of change, yet encouraging innovation wherever this is useful or required. The aim must be to develop a conviction that change is inevitable, but at the same time to try to achieve control over its objectives and influence the manner of its introduction wherever possible.

Activity

Do you encourage change? Do you:

Encourage new ideas and lateral thinking about problems?
Question constructively why things are done in a particular way?
Encourage debate, even if it produces unwelcome ideas?
Draw on past experience without being misled into thinking the past was always better?
Set objectives that involve change?
Make it possible for pilot schemes to be tried?
Develop everyone's skills in managing change?
Support people through change?

Changing Individual Behaviour

Managers must be adept at bringing about changes in individual behaviour. The means of achieving this, as K Blanchard has pointed out, depends on an assessment of both the competence and commitment of the individual concerned. Good managers will adapt their style accordingly:

- A *directive* style – giving very specific instruction – is appropriate where people lack confidence and where commitment may be low, requiring close supervision.
- A *coaching* style is based on clear direction, but with scope for a little more initiative, with less close supervision. This is suitable where the person is keen but inexperienced and as yet lacking in competence.
- A *supporting* style is considered suitable for use with someone who has basic competence but whose performance has declined, probably due to a loss of motivation or confidence.
- A *delegating* style, based on objectives and allowing a high degree of discretion, is more likely to work with competent, well-motivated people.

It is important that when there is some reason to correct staff this is done quickly, privately and very specifically, without making damaging personal judgements on individuals (taken from Blanchard et al. 1985).

Managers of highly performing teams develop people through delegation, also providing guidance, coaching, review and correction.

Staff Development

Staff development activities are powerful ways of generating improved performance. Staff not only become more competent: their motivation is improved, since most staff find their own development intrinsically rewarding. The manager should try to get agreement at senior level to a long-term investment strategy for the department, or failing that, build in a cost element into service pricing to allow for training. Much can be achieved simply by creating the right climate, however.

The value of providing continuous learning opportunities of every kind is one which professional managers need to endorse. Not only does such an approach ensure staff are highly motivated. It also leads to innovation and a professional excellence. It is the best antidote to short term-ism and anti-professionalism that may exist in the organisation. The reputation to cultivate is not is not that 'Our department always wants to send its staff on courses' but rather, 'Our department knows how to use all our training opportunities – we can demonstrate the results' (see Chapter 7).

Summary

The following are important components for a management style which leads to high performance and achievement

Realism

Know what you want to do, and what can be done. That is, be clear about priorities, resources and available options.

Job Clarity and Empowerment

Define job roles and ensure people know exactly what they are required to do and what authority and resources are delegated to do it with. Identify the right skill mix. Be clear about accountability. Set clear objectives.

Staff are empowered by being given the chance to take responsibility and make decisions. Create an atmosphere of problem solving rather than of blame, and make sure of the delivery of what was promised.

Measurement

Identify input, throughput and output requirements. Model the requirements for your own department as a system, by identifying planned outcomes; input, output and throughput requirements; output standards and standards of competence.

Communication and Teamwork

Communication should be open, informative and responsive. Managers need to create the right conditions for teamwork to be effective.

Concern for Quality

This should be stimulated. There are many ways the manager can do this.

Promoting Change

Managers must promote change and help people to adapt to it. They must be adept at bringing about changes in individual behaviour. Diagnosis of problems in terms of competence and motivation will suggest whether a directive, coaching, supporting or delegating style is best. Planned staff development is essential.

Chapter 5

Staff Appraisal Stage by Stage

This chapter discusses the nuts and bolts of conducting appraisal, starting with an analysis of the stages in the process of formal and informal appraisal. It addresses some key issues faced by managers wanting to initiate appraisal within a department:

- choosing the right kind of appraisal
- what the organisation expects
- finding the time
- getting started
- requirements of each stage: preparation, action and paperwork
- who should undertake appraisal
- problems in assessment.

There are many different approaches and organisational practices vary considerably. What is said here should help managers to formulate the approach which best suits them, taking account of the needs of their organisation and staff.

The Cyclical Process of Appraisal

Performance appraisal is a process (usually involving a manager and subordinate) concerned with identifying and assessing performance and development requirements. If we add a supportive element to this, our aims for appraisal might be these:

- clarifying what a person should be doing;
- setting realistic objectives and standards;
- making people aware of future requirements;
- reviewing progress;
- giving support and encouragement;
- getting to know people and assisting their development.

These can all be advanced through the appraisal process. In doing so, the manager will be satisfying important values associated with high levels of achievement and performance that is: realism, job clarity and empowerment, measurement, communication and teamwork, concern for quality and promoting change, which were mentioned in Chapter 4.

Good appraisal is about good feedback (for both parties), recognition, and the chance to resolve difficulties. Even in its simplest form, it offers the manager the chance to reinforce the links between an individual's effort and performance, and the outcomes that result. Figure 5.1 shows a very simple cyclical process of appraisal, incorporating three stages:

1. clarification and planning;
2. monitoring, support, coaching; and
3. progress review.

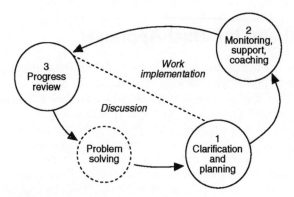

Figure 5.1 Informal appraisal

Stage 1: Clarification and Planning

This is essentially concerned with clarifying what a person should be doing and setting realistic objectives and standards. Here also is the opportunity to give support and encouragement, to get to know people and assist their development. Some informal targets may be set for work or development. Plans are agreed. These may be noted down but there is no formal record of the proceedings. Third parties do not have access to this process or monitor it.

Stage 2: Monitoring, Support and Coaching

This comprises an *implementation* phase where agreed plans are followed up, and the person is given any necessary help. This will involve some guidance and the provision of coaching if required. The timescale of this phase can be anything from a week or two to a few months; it is not usually longer.

Stage 3: Progress Review

This completes the cycle by taking stock of what has been achieved over the period since the Stage 1 discussion. This will involve the recognition of both success and shortfalls in performance and achievement. Where appropriate, problems can be diagnosed. Relevant information is recorded and carried forward into the next Stage 1 discussion, when the cycle starts again. There is no formal assessment, and any report made is not passed on to other parties.

Formal and Informal Appraisal

Our simple model (Figure 5.1) could be called informal appraisal. It is a natural and spontaneous process of clarification, review and problem solving which need have no formalities or documentation. Such a process can be developed in a number of ways, by elaborating the components according to what is required. Thus, *clarifying* what a person should be doing might involve no more than an informal discussion of the person's work, and a discussion of difficulties. A more developed version might involve a detailed discussion of the job role and revisions to the job description. The *planning* part might in a simple form be an agreement to make changes after a problem-solving discussion. In its most complex form it could elaborate complex performance agreements based on organisational requirements, containing 10 or 12 objectives, each with an action plan and appropriate performance indicators. A simple form of *progress* review might be the question: 'How are you getting on?' A more comprehensive approach might involve completion of an elaborately structured set of criteria for assessment, or a structured discussion on the achievement of objectives. Getting to know people and assisting their development can range from informal discussion of immediate needs to structured personal development plans and career development discussions.

Formal appraisal (Figure 5.2) tends to be a highly structured, organisationally coordinated activity, serving multiple purposes. Formal reports are retained, possibly on personal files, and inspected by senior managers and personnel managers. Informal appraisal can be introduced between the formal stages of objective setting and performance review.

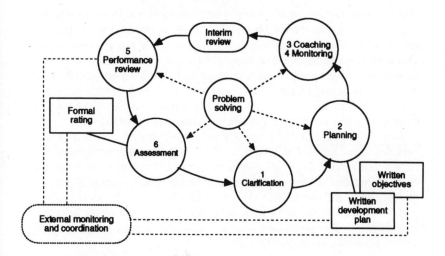

Figure 5.2 Formal appraisal

Choosing the Right Kind of Appraisal

Considerations: For what purposes is appraisal to be used? How much detail, precision and objectivity are appropriate? Should it be formal or informal? Do all staff require the same level and kind of appraisal?

Even if you are forced to operate within the organisation's appraisal scheme, it is worth thinking about what you want from appraisal. Can your needs be met just as well through an informal process? Consider the potential benefits of appraisal:

1. Clarity about what is expected in a job (and how it relates to overall objectives).
2. Feedback for staff on their performance (and appreciation).

3. Identification of problems.
4. Better understanding between manager and member of staff.
5. Identification of training and development needs.
6. Identification of performance priorities.
7. Career planning.
8. A basis for performance assessment (eg, for promotion or pay determination).

One to seven above can all be achieved to some extent through *informal* appraisal. However, it must be said that it will not be possible to plan or assess performance without either setting objectives fairly formally (see Chapters 7, 8 and 9), or using some structured criteria for performance assessment. To properly identify training and development needs, or to do career planning, a structured approach and considerable time are needed. Performance assessment for other purposes calls for the kind of objectivity and rigour that is not likely in informal appraisal.

In an informal appraisal process, where the priority is on the dialogue between manager and subordinate, there may be little or no need for paperwork. It is usually helpful to for both parties to write down what has been agreed, but not for a lot of forms to be filled in. I suggest, however, that agendas will be useful (eg, see page 68). You may come to the conclusion that some staff will respond much better to a more informal appraisal, or that you should combine the two, to provide your staff with a more personal and immediate contact.

Formal schemes are designed to meet a number of organisational purposes. The table below indicates these as well as the percentage of organisations that were found by the Institute of Personnel Management (IPM, now the Institute of Personnel and Development, IPD) in 1985 to incorporate them into their appraisal schemes.

To review past performance	98%
To improve current performance	97%
To assess training/development needs	97%
To set performance objectives	81%
To assess increases or new levels in salary	40%
To assess future potential and promotability	71%
To assist career planning decisions	75%
Other	4%

Appraisal processes have to become formal and involve standardised documentation in order to meet these wider organisational needs. This is the main difference from informal appraisal. Because it may be used to make personnel, training and pay decisions, people unknown to the appraisee have statistical and personal information from the system. The documentation will be used for personnel records, and to enable the whole process to be monitored. It may also be linked to assessment for performance related pay or to an analysis of training needs or identifying people thought to be promotable.

In such organisationally coordinated formal schemes, the scheduling and structure of the meetings is usually fairly prescribed, with lots of standard paperwork. This is meant to help the appraiser, but too frequently affects the participants' control over the process, reducing it to a form-filling exercise to be completed within one month. It also serves as an inhibiting reminder that third parties have an interest in the discussion. In a more formal scheme there is likely to be more information on the performance agreement, some detailed assessment of performance (against objectives or standards) and probably a formal comment from both parties. Appraisees are often asked to sign a form to confirm the meeting and its outcomes (*not* to say they agree with the appraiser's opinion). There is usually space for appraisees to write their own comments beside those of the appraiser.

Monitoring of Formal Appraisal Schemes

This is important, and is usually assigned to the manager's manager (or appraiser's appraiser) frequently known as the 'grandparent', who must ensure the process and procedures are carried out correctly, and follow up any difficulties that emerge. There might be a serious failure to agree, or a feeling of unfairness or discrimination. It may be that the procedures were not being carried out properly, or there is a serious problem in their use. In addition, statistical comparisons of grading and tests of gender bias may be undertaken as part of the monitoring process.

For most people, the difficulty of getting the formal process right is proportional to its complexity. Quite often the structure intended to help appraisers (eg, by including many checklists of questions to be answered) ends up by adding to their burdens. It is likely that this is a reason for the demise of many past schemes.

If you are a manager, it is important not to let the bureaucratic aspects of formal schemes destroy the value of appraisal. Even if the scheme you have to operate has faults, try to identify the parts which will have value for you and your staff.

Finding the Time

Considerations: Who will need to be seen? How many meetings? Is delegation an option? How long will each meeting take? What additional time will be required?

With a very busy workload, and an often exhaustingly wide span of control, many healthcare managers rightly worry about the time they have for appraisal. Where this is a problem, the manager might consider whether some staff should be excluded from the process. This might seem divisive or discriminatory, yet is sometimes inevitable.

Appraisers should assume that there will need to be at least two meetings per year with each member of staff. Normally one of these will be what I have called the clarification and planning meeting and the other the formal review meeting. If we are setting standards, and there is little change in the work role, it is possible than one meeting could suffice. However, where objectives are being set it is far more useful to allow both parties time to consider what is being proposed before it is finalised. To do everything in one meeting might make the person feel 'rail-roaded'. Allow an hour for each of these meetings, and some time for preparation and follow up.

There may be a need for interim, informal appraisal meetings, to check progress. New staff may require more of the appraiser's time. So also might staff who undertake projects and learning assignments. People find that work on personal or career development plans requires separate meetings.

Allow time to think through the details of objectives, to check out the availability of resources, to talk to other members of staff who may be required to offer help, or to check the availability of training opportunities.

Delegation may be an option, although some experts think that appraisal should not be delegated. Consider how important it is for the individual to have your personal involvement, or endorsement, consider also the capability of the person to whom you are thinking of delegating. You do need to monitor the delegation, and have some say in the objectives being set. You must be ready to step in if things go wrong. If you can see your way through these potential difficulties, then delegation may be an option (see Chapter 7).

Starting a Scheme of Appraisal

Considerations: How to phase it in (eg, by staff grouping or by gradually developing the processes); briefing and preparation.

It is not a bad idea to phase in appraisal to let people get used to it. Thus its introduction can be monitored, and teething problems sorted out relatively easily.

Phasing Staff Groups in

Which staff group should start first? In organisations where there are clear hierarchical levels matching status and responsibility, it might make sense to phase in appraisal downwards, one level at a time. For example G and F grade nurses, then E grades, then D grades, and so on. People will normally accept this as reasonable. This matches any downward cascade of objectives. An alternative might be to phase it in section by section, where people work in self contained teams or departments. It is worthwhile briefing those *not* involved, particularly if they are senior, to stem any possible resentment at being missed out initially.

Developing the Process by Stages

Another way of phasing in appraisal is gradually to extend the process. Consider the manager's aims again:

1. clarifying what a person should be doing;
2. setting realistic objectives and standards;
3. making people aware of future requirements;
4. reviewing progress;
5. giving support and encouragement;
6. getting to know people and assisting their development.

If the aim is to cover 1–5 eventually, it may be that 1, 3 and 5 are introduced first, and 2, 4 and 6 added later. It may be that 2 is developed from a relatively simple form to a more sophisticated process as people get used to the idea, or get more experience in setting objectives. The danger in any phasing is that sometimes things get stuck, and no one has the time to get them moving on. This is fatal as far as the development of appraisal is concerned.

Briefing and Preparatory Work

Appraisal will not work unless appraisers and appraisees are fully aware what it is about and have the skills to make it work. Research suggests that training in appraisal is time well spent. Chapter 7 describes the competences and skills that are required by the appraiser.

The people being appraised need to be able to approach it without anxiety and to be confident that they can make use of the opportunity. Many have found short briefing sessions to be of great value. It is probably worth going further than this, training people in setting objectives, for example. It is important that the manager resists the pressure to introduce appraisal too quickly. Before you start you must make sure that everyone is clear about:

- *the purposes* – eg, to provide useful feedback to individuals on their work;
- *what will happen* – eg, each member of staff will have a meeting with their immediate supervisor to discuss and agree some objectives for the coming year;
- *what's required of them* – eg, everyone is asked to prepare by thinking of three objectives they would like to achieve in the coming year;
- *what they are likely to get from it* – this will give you a better idea of how your contribution relates to the work of the department, and the chance to raise any difficulties;
- *when and how it will happen* – eg, it will start in three weeks' time with all senior staff and work through to all staff by 3 September. Everyone will get two weeks' notice of their meetings.

It is important that people have the chance to ask any questions and express any worries at the outset, so that a positive climate for appraisal can develop. Early on the manager should take steps to ensure that people's early experience is productive and not threatening. From the early feedback obtained the manager should be prepared to review and adapt the process to get it right.

Starting the Cycle

It is important that appraisal meetings are planned at least a week in advance. They should be held at times that are convenient to both parties. Although the appraiser may not want them to over run, they should not be sandwiched between other events that mean they become squeezed, truncated or postponed. A good time is later in the day, on a day when there are not too many other commitments for either party. They should be held in a comfortable setting, with no possibility of interruption, except in an emergency.

Look again at Figure 5.2, which develops the simple model of appraisal to cover a *formal* system. Note the main stages of: clarification; planning (objectives and development); performance coaching; monitoring; interim review; full performance review; assessment. Problem solving can be linked to any of these. Note that this is an elaboration of the model of informal appraisal (Figure 5.1). We will look at each stage in turn, to examine the purpose and requirements from the appraiser. The meetings at stages 1 and 2 are described fairly prescriptively here, as are stages 6 and 7. This is because there is often a requirement for formality at these stages, whereas stages 3, 4 and 5 can be carried out a lot more flexibly and informally. Regrettably, these stages are frequently omitted completely. We use the word 'appraiser' and 'appraisee' here, to avoid making assumptions that it is necessarily the person's manager carrying out the appraisal – although it usually will be.

Familiarisation

The appraiser will need to be familiar with the work, abilities and aspirations of the individual. The appraiser needs to think about the future part this person can play in the departmental plans. Hence, certain documents should be studied in advance, and, where useful, brought to meetings:

- local appraisal procedures
- the individual's personal file, training record, job description and achievement plan
- details of the individual's achievements, assignments, projects and team involvement
- details of objectives and standards set previously (and outcomes)
- details of objectives set for other staff
- information collected on the individual's performance
- the manager's own objectives
- organisation charts, departmental and business plans.

The appraiser should also draw up a checklist for each meeting as an aide-mémoire or agenda.

It is an excellent idea for appraiser and staff member to make contact before the initial meeting so the appraiser can explain the purpose and agree a mutually convenient time. The appraiser should stress the value of the meeting and deal with any misconceptions and fears. The appraiser can personally issue and explain any paperwork involved, and ask the person to give some thought to their personal achievements, difficulties and needs.

Stage 1: Clarification

Purpose: To identify performance requirements from now on.

The manager as appraiser will want to mention what is happening in the department and how this impacts on its work. Here is an opportunity to signal priorities and to identify some of the questions that have to be resolved, as well as opportunities for improvements. The impact of important new developments or change in available resources should also be mentioned. This can lead to more detailed planning in stage 2.

The First Time Round

The first time round the appraiser's aims will be to get to know individuals and their work and to help to clarify expectations and deal with any difficulties, ie, to make very general review of progress. The questions below have been helpful in focusing sessions for nurses at D and E grades, and can even be used as an agenda for the very first appraisal meeting at stage 1.

Questionnaire for Staff

1. What is the overall purpose of your job? What are the most important things do you do?
2. What do you feel you have achieved (or successfully overcome) during the year
   in your work?
   in your personal development?
   in other ways?
3. What difficulties do you still have?
4. How has the job changed?
5. What changes in the job would you like to make?
6. What do you feel are your strengths and weaknesses?
7. What extra skills and knowledge would you find helpful?
8. Do you have skills and knowledge that you would like to develop?
9. What objectives would you like to have for the coming year?

This can be used as a kind of agenda for the first stage of appraisal. Question 1 is appropriate for the very first discussion, but it may be omitted next time round. When using this agenda, the appraisee should be encouraged to express their own views, with the appraiser listening and prompting, rather than interrogating. Having first encouraged appraisees to talk, appraisers are then free to raise the issues they need to have discussed.

Changes in the Work Role

A regular task in this clarification stage is to review changes in the work role of the individual. The appraiser should already have some idea on what changes are necessary, and where the individual may need to undertake new activities and perhaps to drop some of the things that are being done currently. Formal confirmation of priorities and (particularly) changes in the work role should be emphasised – not just in the job description, but in assignments, team membership, and competences required.

Clarifying the Psychological Contract

By 'psychological contract' we mean the expectations and obligations that are felt to exist between the organisation and the individual employee. It is important that the manager and staff member can clarify their expectations where it is needed through appraisal. For example:

'I assumed I could take time off when my children are ill.'
'Now that I've shown I can control budgets I'm ready for promotion to ward manager.'
'I think my sickness record is reasonable in the circumstances.'
'I never considered applying for promotion, as I didn't think I had any chance of consideration.'

Personal Development

The development of individuals is linked to the achievements of performance objectives. Mumford (1991) argues for such an opportunistic approach to individual development. The creative manager can set a challenging programme that meets organisational objectives and at the same time provides learning opportunities for the individual (see Chapter 9). What may be difficult is to give enough time to the individual's longer-term development needs within the appraisal discussion itself. That may require a separate meeting or more specialised advice.

The appraiser should consult the individual about their own aspirations, and in particular identify where there are opportunities for development that fit in with the needs of the department. They might involve making the person responsible for something the individual would like to take on or which would develop new competences. Development needs may have been identified in the previous performance review (stage 6). If the appraisee has ambitions to move into a new area or wishes to prepare for senior management roles, the appraiser may need to call in specialist advice. Personal development planning on a wider scale cannot be fitted into a few minutes of the appraisal discussion.

Beware of any temptation to make rash promises or to talk the individual into things that they might later regret. Some of the issues raised here might require further deliberation, or checks on resourcing and support requirements, before being agreed as objectives.

At this point, then, it is useful to summarise, and take stock of what is required, and if appropriate, agree to complete the process at a later meeting. In a few cases, future plans can be drawn up immediately.

Documentation

There is no need to document anything formally. It may be useful to note down the main issues that are discussed and concerns expressed for future reference.

Stage 2: Planning

Purpose: to draw up an agreed achievement plan for the individual.

We are concerned here with these questions:

What objectives or standards are being agreed?
How do they relate to the person's work role and development?
Will any extension of the person's authority be required?
What resources will be required?
Is any training or coaching required?
What sponsorship or support (from the manager or others) is required?
What performance indicators (standards or outcome measures) are to be used to identify achievement?
What is the action plan?

The answers to these questions may be very simple and brief – or they may require a lot of thought and a separate meeting.

Preparation

The appraiser should consider those tasks or result areas where the individual can make a vital or special contribution. What tasks or result areas will provide crucial development opportunities for the individual? Which objectives will the individual be *motivated* to achieve?

Discussion of Objectives and Standards

We must avoid any feeling that set objectives and standards exist separately from work role requirements. Objectives are in fact work role requirements (or personal development needs) that assume a particularly high priority. Six objectives or standards should be the maximum, with one or two as developmental objectives and the others as performance objectives. It is a good idea to include at least one suggested by the appraisee. Setting standards follows the same principles as setting objectives, but is somewhat simpler – there may only be a limited action plan. It is a good idea to attach a time scale for achievement, however. Chapters 7, 8 and 9 cover objective and standard setting in detail within an organisational context.

The appraisee's ideas should be elicited and built on wherever possible. Some of the objectives or standards may not be seen as negotiable in themselves, but there is usually plenty of scope to incorporate the appraisee's views on *how* they are achieved (eg, in drawing up an action plan). Persuade the individual to agree at least one difficult or challenging objective or standard.

Mention and discuss any likely constraints or potential difficulties. Consider and note requirements for time, information, equipment, finance and support. Identify learning needs required by performance objectives, and frame them as individual development objectives where this is appropriate. Make a record of the immediate learning needs and ensure they are included in a personal development plan. Adjourn the meeting and continue later if necessary. Involve the appraisee in developing an action plan for achievement of the objectives.

The appraiser should summarise what has been agreed and put it in writing, ask the appraisee for endorsement within a week, and stress their availability to discuss any queries or difficulties.

Documentation

Everything agreed must be carefully noted. Remember to note agreed changes in the work role. Record objectives in detail as required by the formal appraisal scheme. Specify the review time. You may be required to write down details of performance indicators or measures and action plans as well. This can be useful. Do not forget to record details of resources provided and additional authority to be given, or help promised by the appraiser.

After the Meeting

Ensure that agreed follow up takes place as soon as possible afterwards and that you have the appraisee's endorsement to what has been agreed. Fix diary dates for monitoring meetings and for the final review meeting.

Stage 3: Performance Coaching

Purpose: To equip the individual with appropriate skills and knowledge to meet requirements. To give supportive guidance on performance deficiencies.

Appraisers should learn to see all work experience as a valuable source of learning, and encourage staff to explore this idea in as many ways as possible. Allied to this is the development of self assessment, and of people's ability to learn *how* they best learn.

For many staff the process of agreeing standards and objectives will provide a positive spur to learning. If the opportunity to meet agreed learning requirements is incorporated early on in the appraisal cycle, then a positive approach can be fostered. Thus the contract is:

> 'If I want you to achieve results I must make sure you have the necessary competence and confidence to succeed. So we need to look at your learning needs, and what I as manager/appraiser can do to help.'

If, on the other hand a person is simply allowed to fail – or receive an adverse performance rating – before coaching or training is considered, then any motivation to learn may be destroyed, and the contract between appraiser and appraisee is soured. Even in the most trusting circumstances, some people will find it hard to admit any deficiency, others will be totally unaware of any, or need the payoff to be right before undergoing what may be a painful learning process. All these issues are important in appraisal. In Chapter 6 we consider the skills needed to promote learning, and Chapter 9 gives examples of setting developmental objectives, based on an identification of needs and methods.

Stage 4: Monitoring

Purpose: To set up appropriate feedback systems.

The monitoring method should be explained carefully so that it is understood by all concerned, including how it will relate to any final assessment made. The aim should be to provide feedback frequently, based on complete and up-to-date information from different sources. The information used should be freely available, with self-monitoring being encouraged as much as possible. It may involve reports by independent observers or increasing individuals' own awareness of key signals which they can use to guide their performance.

Stage 5: Interim Performance Review

Purpose: To give feedback to the individual on progress so that adjustments can be made.

It is extremely valuable to individuals to know they are on course. It is surely unforgivable to allow an individual to go wrong because no one bothered to say anything until it was too late. If interim review meetings are carefully structured, and both parties are organised (above all in having access to the right information), they may not be too time consuming. True, there will be a need to allow time to sort out problems, but this may be minor compared to the time spent retrieving some project that has gone badly wrong. The subtext might be: 'Are we on target? What is the deviation? Is it important? What's causing it? How do we put it right?' If you are thinking that interim reviews are simply part of good everyday management practice – you are right!

Stage 6: Full Performance Review

Purpose: to review what was expected (by both parties) and what has been achieved.

What was expected?
We must know what agreed commitments were made earlier at stage 2. There may be difficulties if these have not been written down.

What has been achieved?
This is a very important part of the appraisal discussion. Both parties must assemble an agreed picture of what was achieved and what not. This is partly factual, and partly about feelings and expectations. Certainly the review is a source of learning (by reflection and discussion). Often it provides the evidence for assessment as well.

Currently the focus is less on reviewing past performance and towards development and improvement. However, the past cannot be ignored completely for four good reasons. First, there is a need to review and agree about past outcomes if the process of objective- and standard-setting is to have credibility. Secondly, past performance deficiencies may persist unless some diagnosis is undertaken. Thirdly, the appraisal discussion provides a means of recognition of effort and achievement by the manager. Lastly, performance pay and other rewards are based on retrospective achievement. One needs to adopt a 'water under the bridge' attitude to things which may have occurred in the past but which are now no longer important issues. For example: 'In January last year the individual was new to the job and performance reflected this', or 'In August he had personal difficulties, but such a bad patch is unlikely to reoccur'.

Useful Techniques For Reviewing

If the appraiser has been reviewing the performance throughout the year, there should be no surprises here. This sequence of questions works well.

1. What went well – and why?
2. What did not go well – and why?
3. If you had to do it again what would you do differently – and why?
4. What action do you/we need to take?

In a review we concentrate on questions 1 and 2 to begin with; 3 might then provide a basis for reflecting on what can be learnt; and 4 might be part of a personal development plan. The appraiser asks for the appraisee's answers before giving her own. Refer to factual data wherever possible. It is the appraiser's task to increase the appraisee's self awareness and commitment to improvement. Recognise success and build on it, without allowing complacency to set in.

With success we are on fairly safe ground. Even if the person is aware of it already, the appraiser's recognition of it during the appraisal discussion is still important – particularly if there are some less successful areas as well. If we are to build on successes it is useful to identify what went well, together with the conditions that led to it.

Do not raise issues that should have come up in earlier reviews, or introduce new success criteria. The appraisee is not likely to respond well to an appraiser saving up criticisms in order to have something to say on the day of the formal review in the appraisal. The reaction is likely to be: 'If only I had known that I was not coming up to standard earlier, I could have done something about it!' The appraiser is looking here for recognition of a shortfall – not a judgement on the individual.

Annual formal reviews are often unsatisfactory. In practice, a year may be too long a time span for formal performance review, where objectives are achieved quicker. The time of year set for mass reviews by the organisation may be inappropriate. Appraisers might want to negotiate some scope to undertake reviews earlier than the set date for submission of paperwork. It is vital that performance reviews are seen as worthwhile and meaningful, and worth taking the trouble to prevent a cynical attitude towards them. It is a question of getting the right balance between organisational requirements and meeting local needs, which can be difficult.

Documentation

Indicate whether objectives were met. Give relevant factual and quantitative information. Mention obvious causes of failure. Avoid subjectivity, although give credit for effort and achievement where it is due.

Addressing Problems

Outstanding difficulties may require exploration and resolution before future objectives can be set. The appraiser (or the appraisee) may want to explore the reasons for any shortfalls, and analyse causes, when the shortfall has major impact on the work, or when there is some emotional block or distress which is preventing the person from moving on. It is needed when the failure is likely to reoccur or cause difficulties again in future and when the appraisee is likely to learn a great deal from the analysis. Recognition of problem areas works best when led by the appraisee. Do not overdo the critical analysis, though. Some things are better left unsaid.

The appraiser should as far as possible adopt a joint problem-solving approach which refers to specific actions and behaviour rather than suggests some general weakness on the part of the individual. This allows for the maximum self-assessment and at the same time offers support and affirmation to the individual where necessary. Past mistakes are treated as something to be learned from, and not as evidence of incapability. In this way, intentions for change or improvement are reinforced.

Sometimes, however skilled and persistent the appraiser is, there will be reluctance on the part of the appraisee to accept that there is any problem at all. Expect some denial if a rating determining a level of reward is to be made on the basis of alleged success or failure. The reason for any shortfall may be attributed to others or the shortfall may simply not be acknowledged. In this case the discussion may need to be continued elsewhere. Sometimes major problems emerge that will require a concerted remedial strategy. There are also people who consistently undervalue their own performance.

Working up Solutions

If a shortfall is important enough to require some plan for its correction, some development or performance objectives can be agreed. Any problem or deficiency in the manager's court should be attended to promptly, and reported back on. Appraisers should consider carefully how much of the discussion to record. All commitments should be noted, however.

Stage 7: Assessment

Purpose: to identify how the person has performed overall.

The staff member should have been made aware of the basis used for any assessment; have been given notice of the consequences of failing to meet requirements, and have had early warning of shortfalls in performance. This is particularly important if assessments are going to affect opportunities and material rewards provided.

Appraisers rating staff performance must have clearly and objectively identified their criteria for assessment, and the evidence they plan to use (eg, behavioural definitions of effective performance) before making the assessment. Where the assessment is to be used to determine reward, the appraiser can expect disagreement and differences of opinion.

What to Write

Ratings must where possible refer to set criteria, objective evidence, standards and norms. This means identifying whether above or below the average, or required standard, and specific details of shortfalls in performance (maybe as percentages or frequencies). This assumes we know what the average or required standard is. Some examples of performance ratings are shown below.

Examples of Performance Ratings

ACCURACY/QUALITY
Is the work produced accurate? Are errors a frequent occurrence? Is work completed to a high quality?
Above average rate of error, particularly in figure work.

MEETING DEADLINES
Can the appraisee work to tight deadlines and cope with high workloads while maintaining a high degree of accuracy and quality?
Generally meets deadlines in own work (95 per cent), but unwilling to respond to others' demands for extra effort.

COMMUNICATION
Is the appraisee able to communicate effectively orally? Is written work completed to a high standard and with the required range and depth of thought?
Oral communication satisfactory. Some deficiency in written work: report writing is below required standard owing to poor structuring and a tendency not to provide enough specific detail.

DECISION MAKING
Is the appraisee able to make and take decisions? Are decisions made on the basis of the best available information and with the required consultation? Are decisions made of a high quality and do they demonstrate sound judgement?
Sound judgement shown in own area of expertise. Frequently fails to take account of other people's priorities (three examples) – this has been confirmed by two close associates.

Assessment will not support learning if it is handled badly; in other words, if the feedback is based mainly on negative criticisms that lead to a demotivation of the appraisee, where any learning opportunities are rejected. On the other hand, we know that some appraisers do not want to be critical at all, and this is also unlikely to bring about learning. If learning is to take place, then there has to be a pay-off for the appraisee in being frank and open, and he or she must feel motivated to take it on board. Any comments made should point to improvements and lead to a plan for development. These issues are dealt with in more depth in the next chapter.

Combining Meetings

If we are not to end up with three or four meetings with every individual, we will need to combine certain stages in the appraisal process. Stages 1 and 2 can be brought together; so can stages 6 and 7. If requirements are very simple, it might be possible to lump all these stages together (ie, 6 and 7 – first cycle, with 1 and 2 – second cycle).

If you are agreeing objectives, I recommend that you adjourn the discussion after there has been a preliminary discussion of future expectations and possible objectives (ie, at the beginning of stage 2). This will enable both parties to give consideration to the shape of the achievement plan.

Appraisal in Practice

Despite the many supposed advantages of the appraisal process, in many healthcare organisations there is frequently a very mixed reaction to the idea. Traditionally in the NHS people have seen it variously as little more than an unwelcome annual interview, a stressful confrontation between staff and managers, a threatening trial where unfair judgments are made, an inconsequential conversation, or a rather pointless bureaucratic ritual required by the personnel department. Over the years there have been national schemes for nurses, administrators, senior managers, and countless local initiatives, some of which thrive, but many of which have long since been abandoned. Here are some typical comments.

> 'Appraisal was started once and seemed a good idea at the time, but after the initial enthusiasm it just faded out. All I remember was a lot of paperwork. I had to put down some objectives, but they were never followed up – were all busy at the time and the manager kept having to cancel the meetings.'

> 'I don't agree with it. I certainly don't want to have to rate my staff performance – that will lead to jealousies. In any case they all do a reasonable job. If they didn't they'd soon hear about it. It would take up far too much of my time.'

> 'My manager once had a chat which she called an appraisal discussion. She didn't seem to know what she was doing, and we never really got down to any of the nitty gritty.'

> 'I know that in one place it seemed to be part of the disciplinary process, and they had to call the union in because people were so afraid to see their manager. Eventually they had so much trouble with people refusing to attend that they scrapped it altogether.'

> 'I wish someone would tell me how I am doing sometimes, give me some encouragement...'

Some Critical Issues in Appraisal

Ideally, the appraisal discussion should be a rich and private interaction where both parties can have their say and get to know each other. It reinforces the manager's role, recognises the value of the employee's contribution and builds the relationship. Done well, it improves motivation and commitment as nothing else can. The employee should usually come away reassured and regenerated.

Unfortunately, in many organisations appraisal has become swamped by the requirements placed on it, such as the rating of performance for allocation of performance pay, and the identification of promotables. These requirements tend to block constructive discussions of development needs. Appraisal is often seen as a set of paperwork procedures, owned by the personnel department, and of little value to the manager.

An IPM survey (1992) showed that 80 per cent of organisations were dissatisfied with their appraisal systems. So how does one make a success of it? Below are some crucial issues.

Who should Undertake Appraisal Interviews?

Must appraisal be undertaken by the immediate manager? In theory, the answer is 'yes' for several good reasons. The manager needs to develop a personal relationship with the individual, to identify requirements and enter into agreements for achievement and development. In any case, managers cannot delegate their *overall* responsibility for the employee's performance, and therefore for appraising staff. Besides this, the individual may feel sold short if someone else becomes involved as a kind of 'locum'. Such a person might have difficulty in agreeing an acceptable performance plan at a distance from the person with the authority to make decisions. Despite these problems, there are good reasons why delegation has to happen sometimes.

If appraisal is to be carried out by proxy, there are some fairly demanding requirements if it is to be effective and not to lead to confusion. Managers delegating appraisal must, in some way, personally endorse the objectives together with any delegation of work, and confirm any assessment of performance made. The appraisee must have access to the manager when required. The role delegated to the proxy appraiser, and any authority that goes with it, must be very clear. This role is facilitating rather than executive – ie, mainly helping work out details, and giving support. The proxy must supervise the appraisee's work (giving feedback) and must also be competent to undertake a supportive coaching role. There might be correspondingly more emphasis on self appraisal and appraisal by others.

Appraisal by Managers from Different Professions

Occasionally concern is expressed when it is necessary for people to be appraised by managers who do not share the professional or technical training of those whom they appraise. Although sensitive, this is possible provided that the manager observes the ground rules. The unqualified manager should not attempt to make assessments of performance in professional areas. Professional help should be sought when agreeing professional work role requirements and in monitoring achievement plans requiring the exercise of professional competences, and in areas of professional development.

This could be a minefield if there is a climate of distrust. It will not be fair for the manager concerned to delegate the assessment of professional competence to another subordinate, unless this is part of a personal development plan. So the strategies available to the manager are: to leave assessment and development of professional competence out of the appraisal process altogether, *or* to engage someone else competent to do it (such as a professional supervisor) and in effect have two separate ratings and achievement plans, *or* to work jointly throughout with a professionally qualified assessor, *or* to use the services of a professional coach or mentor.

The third option is often used, supplemented by the fourth: it has the advantage of maintaining the integrity of the overall achievement plan, and allowing the right kind of input into the achievement plan and personal development plan. All parties must be happy with the arrangements decided on.

These issues are less sensitive where appraisal is based on development. Where PRP is at stake, it is far more sensitive, and options one or two may be preferred.

Appraisal by Others

Some organisations are developing appraisal systems that require peers or subordinates to appraise ('upward' appraisal). Fletcher (1993) says this can be useful provided it is done anonymously and in areas where peers or subordinates are qualified to make judgements. For example, subordinates might assess bosses' delegation skills but not their management potential.

Successful Assessment

Merit Rating

People being examined by their superiors in order for their deficiencies to be determined is still very much part of professional educational practice. Line managers often dislike criticising subordinates to their face, and even where they have the necessary skills, they may distrust the validity of the scheme they have to use. Nevertheless, although on the decline, merit assessment is still very much alive in many performance appraisal schemes. Some of these rate people on merit on a range from 'outstanding' to 'unsatisfactory', on a number of dimensions considered relevant. These may range from subjective character ratings (regarded as of little value) to those which are behaviourally anchored and extensively validated. Such ratings are used in assessment centres, commonly when posts are reorganised, and in development centres to identify development needs. The practice of merit rating is especially difficult when linked to pay, or where the rating has a bearing on future outcomes for the individual (such as job security, training or promotion).

Even where professionals resist the idea of 'A to E' ratings for all staff on the grounds that it is unnecessary, divisive, or impossible, most accept the idea of giving feedback to staff (particularly novices) on whether they were achieving the required performance or competency – although Alan Fowler (1990) doubts whether merit rating has ever improved performance. At best, it is notoriously prone to bias.

Rating Based on Achievement

The search for other relevant measures of performance led to the idea of setting measurable targets, and to the use of *objectives* (see Chapter 1). Several questions then arise. Is the measure used to indicate the achievement of the objective adequate as a measure of individual performance? What other factors have played a part in the achievement? What other criteria are important to assess? Do we need to assess *how* the person has achieved objectives as well as *what* has been achieved? How do we assess someone who has achieved some but not all objectives? For example, The Magpies' Cricket Club does not gives annual awards to the best players but to the most *improved* ones. So each player, no matter how untalented, has a chance to demonstrate improvement on last year's performance. The most improved players win cups, which clearly puts a premium on improvement through effort rather than ability. Should performance rating work that way – to be a stimulus for development? Or must we bear in mind the market for talent, and reward the really high achievers to maintain their commitment?

The answer is that a scheme can be weighted either way, but we must be consistent about it, and recognise that the impact of each strategy for the organisation in the long run will be different. The answers relate to the kind of achievement culture that we want to foster (eg, competitive/meritocratic or developmental/supportive). Do we want to encourages the high-fliers or encourage general self-improvement across the board?

Does Performance Assessment Lead to Performance Improvement?

It would be nice to think that in a below par performance the process of assessment would be the spur to a constructive discussion about improvements and a remotivation of the individual. Peters and Waterman (1982) say that we should not fight shy of performance assessment, since it is a vital component of a culture where constructive criticism and risk taking is welcomed. They claim that in high performing organisations, 'people like to compare themselves to others... they also like to perform against standards'. The supposed motivating power of setting high expectations is more important that being certain that every judgement is absolutely equitable.

While it is legitimate for bosses to form and express an opinion of their subordinates' work performance, and to express it to them, the business of ratings often appears to undermine motivation. This was the finding of a classic study by Meyer (1965). In reality, assessment is far more likely to *endanger* commitment and generate suspicion unless we can create a climate where criticism is welcomed. Other studies have shown that to have a positive influence, feedback has to be specific, in limited areas, balanced by positive comments, and available from a variety of sources. Participation and self assessment help (see Fletcher, 1981, 1993). Feedback can lead to improvement when trust is high and the individual is very keen to develop. Many experts believe that if we want feedback to be utilised for development, our assessments should not be used to determine personal rewards.

Why Ratings can be Unacceptable

Subjectivity in ratings will give rise to distrust. Ratings will often be challenged when the relationship between appraiser and appraisee is one of personal distrust or when the rater is not familiar with the appraisee's work, or is not considered by the appraisee to have the competence, experience or values to make ratings. In many organisational cultures, defensive reactions can be expected when ratings have negative personal outcomes for individuals, where ratings mean that one individual gains at another's expense or where some individuals can get good ratings by manipulating the system. People will be demotivated when ratings are changed to match a required statistical distribution or when the process does not offer the appraisee development opportunities. The more of these factors that apply, and the more evident each one is, the more demotivating the rating scheme is likely to be.

In other words, ratings will be unacceptable to individuals when they do not feel they have enough *control* or do not feel that the system is *fair* (eg, when the validity or relevance of the scheme and criteria is not accepted). This will be aggravated when assessments can have personally adverse impact. Consultation may indicate what is acceptable. For example, a group performance bonus scheme for exceeding contract targets may be perceived as more acceptable than an attempt to introduce sophisticated criteria for professional contributions into individual performance rating. Technically *fairness* can be improved by using behaviourally anchored criteria or by rating achievement of assessable objectives instead of rating employee characteristics. Reliability is improved by using statistical tests of rater reliability and consistency, by monitoring results for sex, race or other bias, by having ratings monitored by others, and by training assessors.

Improving *control* is difficult for many healthcare staff in that individual work is hard to measure, and a whole range of other people contribute to work results. If we restrict what we measure to what the individual has *total control* over, then we may not be measuring anything very important. If there are differences between the level of control that individual staff have, then differences in results will easily be put down to that factor and not to their relative performance. Here are some suggestions for maximising individuals' control.

1. Make sure that objectives are set within the *discretion* (and also the resources, power, competence) of individuals to achieve the outcomes.
2. When control over results is removed from the individual, *amend* the objective (or sufficiently increase the discretion).
3. Set *standards* rather than objectives for staff who lack discretion in their work roles (these may be based on competencies).
4. Encourage *self-appraisal*.

Openness

Criteria must be open, in the sense that they are visible, with no part of the process kept secret from participants. Success criteria should be discussed and agreed fully when set. Payment of rewards for achievement can easily discourage openness. Randell *et al.* (1984) suggested that salary review and performance review should be separated by six months, so that the time between performance and salary reviews could then enable an improvement plan to take effect. A research report from the Management Consultants, Superboss Ltd, mentions 18 key factors for success in formal appraisal, among them: 'The scheme must solely be focused on personal development (personal improvement, development of competencies, identification of training needs, etc); the appraisal must not, in any way, be judgmental (ie, have any form of ratings) or be linked to pay.'

Summary

In choosing the type of appraisal managers should consider its purpose. Many managers will be required to use an organisational scheme, and should be aware of its format, purposes and constraints. The manager needs to consider who needs to be seen, how many meetings are required, and whether delegation might be an option. Briefing of staff is important: everyone must be clear about the purposes; what will happen; what's required of them; what they are likely to get from it; and when and how it will happen.

Formal appraisal involves the following stages, some of which may be combined:

1. Clarification
2. Planning (objectives and development)
3. Performance coaching
4. Monitoring
5. Interim performance review
6. Full performance review
7. Assessment.

Problem solving can be linked to any of these.

Problems with assessment arise from giving merit ratings and ratings on achievement of objectives. If felt to be unacceptable, it will prevent feedback from leading to performance improvement. The problem can be overcome if assessment embodies specificity in feedback, control over performance and benefit to the individual.

Chapter 6

The Complete Appraiser

This chapter explores the role of the appraiser and the competences required to be effective. The roles are related to the overall management responsibilities of the individual undertaking appraisal in a healthcare context, and are summarised as sponsor, monitor and support roles. There are also identifiable competences required in appraisal. They include those of listening, interviewing, assessment, influencing, problem solving and performance planning, which are useful for both parties in appraisal, and coaching, delegation and giving feedback, which relate to managerial aspects.

In the context of healthcare, the power of staff appraisal, and much of its difficulty, come from the need for the manager undertaking it to combine three roles, all of general importance for managing staff well.

Sponsor Role

One of the most important roles the manager has to play is that of sponsor. The manager has accountability for getting certain results. The manager is the agent of the employer and the employee is the agent of the manager. The manager makes staff accountable for work which contributes to the results the manager is charged with achieving. The manager, although not necessarily having hired the person for the job being done, must take responsibility for the individual's success and failure.

The manager must able to plan, establish and reinforce this relationship, as a kind of contract based on meeting standards or agreed objectives. If we like to operate through consent, there is some scope for negotiation about what the contract should be. Nevertheless, the manager does have the right to tell the person what to do – or what not to do, and also to ensure the person has the necessary authority and resources to carry out the work required. The manager therefore has the right to give an opinion on the employee's performance.

Staff are entrusted with responsibility to achieve results, and empowered to do so by the manager. The notion of sponsorship implies a commitment to underwrite the employee's performance, welfare, status and authority. The employee in return agrees to meet the expectations laid on him or her in respect of work and conduct. Appraisal thus supports the psychological contract. Ultimately, if the contract fails, the manager is entitled to take disciplinary action, and even to end the contract – normally subject to approval by a more senior manager. Disciplinary action is the exceptional situation, where there is a need to restore the contract and the relationship.

Appraisal provides the opportunity to *create the working contract* in the first place and to *reinforce* it and *adapt* it. The manager has to brief the appraisee on what is required and on 'what matters'. It would be wrong to play down this aspect of appraisal. The allocation of work, however it is achieved, and the commitments that derive from it, are essential parts of the appraisal process.

Monitor Role

The second important role involves review, assessment and correction. The manager must set standards and objectives, and has the right to judge and decide the quality of people's work contributions; whether results and standards are being achieved as well as the remedies for shortfalls that have been identified. This role can be seen as part of the cyclical management process: it is the 'control loop' that is the basis for clarifying and adjusting expectations and requirements.

Very few people like making judgements, particularly when there may be adverse outcomes for a member of staff with whom the manager has to continue to work. Nevertheless, it is central to the performance improvement process and cannot be evaded. Regular contact will enable problems to be raised, discussed and easily corrected.

With the very large spans of control and spread-out locations that are now common in healthcare, it can be difficult to ensure the monitoring is regular, particularly for some part-time staff. Another difficulty is the diffidence monitors feel about checking up on people 'behind their back', but this is often necessary to get a full picture of the impact of someone's performance.

Support Role

Support for the individual is an important ingredient of appraisal. The role is crucial if we want to develop the individual's confidence and a trusting relationship with the manager. Appraisal may be used to help build team solidarity and mutual support, especially at times of insecurity. Individuals' objectives and action plans will help them adapt to change, maintain influence over what happens to them and even plan their exit if this is necessary.

There is a need to ensure that staff feel supported in very practical ways. Where there are difficulties, even when staff make mistakes, they look to their manager to 'stick up for them'. It may mean, for example, relieving someone when it seems that they have had enough, or in ensuring that their authority, or competence, is made evident to others. It might mean providing extra resources, or reassuring someone who has just been through a bad patch.

There are real difficulties in the idea of the manager as counsellor to staff, because the relationship *must* be constrained by the need the manager has to make judgements about individuals and ultimately to take sanctions against them. This threatens the credibility of any attempt by the manager to present themself as an impartial counsellor.

The support role in appraisal might be demonstrated by the positive comments staff sometimes make: 'We got to understand each other a bit better'; 'I didn't realise before that the manager rates my work so highly'; 'I realise what her priorities are now, I didn't before'; 'I'm glad my manager made time to discuss my problems'; 'I now know where I've been going wrong'; 'We made a plan for my development – she'll support me if I put the work in'.

A negative appraisal experience might evoke the following comments: 'I'm still not clear what he wants from me'; 'I think her criticisms of me were unreasonable'; 'She reckoned I was to blame, but I told her it was really her fault'; 'I never got the chance to say what I wanted to'; 'I don't think she's really being honest with me'; 'We talked about training but I don't believe it'll ever happen'.

Undoubtedly, the appraisal process involves considering difficult issues, recognising shortfalls, accepting ownership of problems, making commitments to change – all of which may be very painful. The manager must have the skills to provide the necessary support for this. In any appraisal situation there are likely to be issues of managing people's feelings, and it is important that the manager is able to foster self-awareness, personal autonomy and trust. Managers must be honest about their own feelings and not allow negative feelings and reactions to damage relationships.

A rather more specialised type of support is needed in a mentor or coaching role, which requires specific competences, concerned with giving reinforcement and encouraging reflection on people's experiences. This will involve the powerful technique of supportive confrontation, where the individual's behaviour may be challenged without loss of rapport or trust (see Figure 6.1).

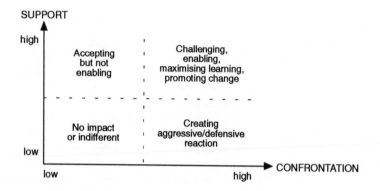

Figure 6.1 Impact of different combinations of support and confrontation

The manager's preferred style, the nature of the work, the organisational culture, the needs of the individual and the relationship will also affect the balance of roles but they will all be required at some point or the manager will not be doing his or her job. If performed effectively, staff will know their work is valued and they will be clearer about what is required from them. They will feel more enthusiasm about their work, and confidence in themselves and their bosses.

Nine Key Competences for Conducting Appraisals

In the appraisal meeting it is important that the manager feels able to be open and to carry out each of the roles when required with skill and without anxiety. The key competences are:

1. Listening
2. Interviewing
3. Assessment
4. Influencing

5. Problem solving
6. Performance planning
7. Coaching
8. Delegation
9. Giving feedback.

1. Listening

Good listening is very difficult. Things that get in the way include: feeling self-conscious about being the listener; losing concentration and thinking about other things; being too busy rehearsing what you want to say; starting to evaluate what is being said; and outside noise or distractions.

If you try to concentrate for five minutes on what someone is saying, and try to repeat back to them *exactly* what they've said, you may notice that: you have forgotten quite a lot of what was said; you have only heard what you wanted to hear and give a slanted version; you have introduced your own feelings into your account; or instead of reporting it verbatim, you have incorrectly paraphrased what has been said.

To prevent these internal and external distractions, it is important to give the speaker your full attention, and to concentrate. Suppress your own feelings or responses and resist the temptation to evaluate. This means keeping separate your feelings for the speaker from those you have about the message. Do not make assumptions about what is going to be said. Ensure your understanding by asking for clarification, or by asking the speaker to slow down, or repeat if necessary. Check your understanding by summarising or paraphrasing and allowing the speaker to confirm or correct, but avoid any desire to interrupt the speaker.

2. Interviewing

In general, at an appraisal discussion, we want to be able to develop information and rapport – while making sure we have adequate control. Each of skills below contribute to one or other of these aims.

Structuring
Plan the use of the discussion time. Be clear what you want to explore. Meet in comfortable surroundings, free from interruptions. Explain the structure of the discussion to the appraisee, and do your best to keep to it. If you need more time, schedule another meeting.

Establishing Rapport
It helps to sit diagonally across from the appraisee rather than opposite, which can appear more confrontational. You may not want the meeting

to become too informal. If you know the individual well and there is a danger of flippancy, you may want to emphasise the structure more. If the individual is nervous, make sure that you encourage the contributions made. Start with unthreatening subjects, and note any signs of anxiety in speech and body language. Show that you are listening by nodding, smiling and engaging in comfortable eye contact. Get a clear idea of the appraisee's opinions and feelings before introducing your own. Sometimes in trying to show empathy, the manager starts to 'lead' the appraisee, or complete the appraisee's sentences. Do not introduce judgements inappropriately or prematurely.

A: This hasn't been a very successful period for you, has it?
B: Oh, I wouldn't say that. I've certainly had some... (pause)
A: Problems?
B: No, I was going to say successes...

Better is an approach that encourages reflection:

A: How do you feel about the last few months?
B: Unsure
A: In what way... ? How have you felt about the work you have done?
B: I've found it difficult at times.
A: Can you say why... ?

Awareness of non-verbal clues, and sensitive synchronisation of eye contact, speech patterns, hand signals and postural patterns, are important here.

Developing Information

The skills are the same as those used in selection interviewing, using sequences of open questions (ones that cannot be answered with 'yes' or 'no'). Here the manager is discussing the appraisee's attempts to interview patients for a survey.

A: How did you find it?
B: Not too bad once I got started.
A: What difficulties were there?
B: Some people just wouldn't stop. Others wanted to tell you about things that weren't relevant. Some assumed you were diagnosing their ailments.
A: How did you deal with that?
B: We decided to give people more information to begin with.
A: What form did that take?
B: We produced a leaflet explaining what we were doing. We had 200 printed and left them in the surgeries.

A: That solved the problem?
B: Yes.
A: Was that the *only* problem?

Note that at the end a closed question: 'That solved the problem?' closed down the appraisee, and 'Was that the *only* problem?' is an exhaustive probe question useful in making sure every stone has been turned.

Summarising and Paraphrasing
These are characteristic of skilful performance. They both help to clarify the point being discussed, can progress the discussion, and give evidence that the manager has been listening. Here the manager summarises the problems expressed in order to move on to exploring possible solutions.

A: We've established that you still have problems with the physical procedures, and that you need to build up your confidence. You appear to understand the theoretical side adequately. That might suggest giving you some supervised practice – or further practical training.

If the appraisee is saying:

B: I still can't feel completely confident doing this on my own. When I'm under pressure I tend to go to pieces, but when there is nobody watching and plenty of time, I can get it right straight away. I know I ought to have no problems by now, but I do.

The appraiser may want to paraphrase like this:

A: You are saying, perhaps, that if you could feel more relaxed, there would be no problem?

Not like this:

A: You are saying we should give you more chance to learn to do it under pressure?

Exploring Difficulties
The manager might need gently to raise awareness and invite the appraisee to explore the causes. The following example is about difficulties the person has in undertaking some procedures without supervision.

A: Do you see why it is important to get this right?
B: Not really, I must admit...
A: Well, perhaps if you were on your own, say at night...
B: Without experienced people around...
A: Yes.
B: OK, I see what you mean, but I'm still not sure why I'm failing...

A: Will it be useful to spend some time exploring that?
B: I think so.
A: What factors might be important?
B: My difficulty with the technical procedures, perhaps. It might be partly about self-confidence.
A: Go on…. Any others?

Note the use of the exhaustive probe question again at the end.

Use of Confrontation

Some confrontation might be needed – this should be exploratory and supportive:

A: You said that you had difficulty with technical procedures – but just now you said that you felt very capable in all areas? Might this be an area for development?

rather than accusatory and judgmental:

A: So much for your comments about your capability! You shouldn't be so cock sure of yourself!

Clarifying

Exploratory confrontation can be used to clarify, as in the above example. It can be done by using a closed question, ie one that calls for a set answer, usually 'yes' or 'no'; for example: 'Was that enjoyable?'; 'Are you telling me that you are no longer interested in working with GPs?'; 'Was it difficult for you to go back on that ward?'; 'Was it because things had changed a lot?'

Supporting and Confirming the Individual's Worth

Reassurance may be needed: 'I don't see that as a problem at all – you coped very well the other day'. Weaknesses might need to be put into the right perspective: 'I have absolute confidence that you will make the grade eventually, but there are one or two areas you need to work on right now'. (The term 'development need' is more affirmative than weakness.)

Proposing and Building

It is better to get the individual to make proposals, but the manager must be ready to build on the proposal.

A: What would you like to take on next?
B: I would like the chance to show what I could do with students.
A: OK – perhaps you could get some practice in with the care assistants?

3. Assessment

The skilful assessor uses factual evidence to interpret criteria in a consistent fashion, ensuring an appropriate spread of ratings. The problems people have in doing this have been well researched.

Subjectivity and Prejudice
Different appraisers come to different conclusions based on the same data, because they have different values, different likes and dislikes. Sex and race prejudice are common, for example.

Central Tendency
Appraisers avoid giving extreme marks or opinions, tending to 'water down' their assessment. Typically, numbers in the 'outstanding' or 'unsatisfactory' categories are disproportionately low. Research suggests that this problem, which is known as the 'central tendency' error, may occur because extreme scores give rather strong signals. Lack of confidence and the inability to discriminate at extreme ends of the scales probably also have an influence.

Leniency
Many, but not all, appraisers like to rate people as 'satisfactory' or better. More than one company on reviewing its assessment practice had to tell people getting satisfactory ratings for years that they had in fact been underachieving.

Halo Effect
Here someone who rates high on one aspect is, without justification, rated high on others as well. The opposite (the 'horns effect') is also found, where an individual scoring low on one aspect is also marked down on others.

Recency Effect
Appraisers put too much weight on the most recent behaviour.

Contrast Effect
This occurs where an individual's rating is distorted by being contrasted with another person's, rather than applying the criteria independently. This may be someone else's rating (or the assessor's self-rating!). The impact might be, for instance, that if there is an outstandingly highly rated individual in a group, the rating of others may be lower than they would be if judged correctly on the criteria.

Other Factors Affecting Ratings

It is common for people to rate themselves higher that their boss does. Thus self-rating can lead to discontent, unless the criteria are understood. Research into ratings in the US showed that raters are less willing or likely to differentiate between the performance of individuals when the purpose is salary or promotion decisions. Raters are more likely to manipulate ratings when political factors are operating in the organisation. Raters give higher ratings to those they like: their moods can also affect ratings.

4. Influencing

At different parts of the appraisal process, control may pass from one party to another. The manager may want to present the 'facts of life' – but appraisees may feel the need to be equally robust, over things they feel are unsatisfactory. Here, the manager will need to be able to make a case; say what he or she wants; express feelings and opinions; and apply incentives and pressures when required. At other times the influencing process will not so much require asserting opinions as working out a mutually acceptable solution to a problem. Here the most appropriate influencing style will be one that involves listening, exploring common ground and consensus building.

5. Problem Solving

Problem solving is at the centre of Figures 5.1 and 5.2 (pages 59 and 61), because appraisal meetings, formal and informal, are for problem solving as much as they are for planning and review.

Who has the Problem?

There is a danger that if we are not careful we can get into 'blame–counter-blame' tactics here. It is often best for the manager to state his or her requirement honestly and unequivocally, and follow a contracting pattern such as:

> 'I need to be sure that I can rely on you to do this task promptly and accurately in future.'
> 'What might prevent that from happening?'
> 'Can we see how we can make sure it happens?'
> 'What will that require on your part – and how can I help you?'

What Kind of Problem?

It will often be necessary to recognise the nature of the problem and to pursue appropriate tactics.

- *Educative* – where the appraisee needs to understand more. In this case, probing skills are useful. A mixture of open and specific questions is used to explore the problem here and define it more clearly. 'Why is it a problem?', 'Is it getting worse?', 'Is it urgent – or serious?', are important questions.
- *Diagnostic* – where the appraisee needs to understand the cause. This is where a scientific approach is called for which might involve a series of stages: state the problem; collect information; list possible causes; generate solutions; evaluate solutions; decide on preferred solution; devise action plan; test it.
- *Decisional* – the person needs to know what course of action to take. Here the sequence might be: state the problem; collect information; list the criteria that need to be met (essential and desirable – or as weightings); generate solutions; evaluate solutions against criteria; decide on preferred solution; devise action plan; test it.
- *Anticipatory* – where we want to make sure things will not go wrong. Here it is useful to draw a flow chart or systems diagram, and to identify each point where there may be a problem. Solutions may involve, for example: ensuring time for piloting and testing; having fall back options.

6. Performance Planning

There is much in Chapters 4, 7 and 8 about the technical basis of planning and measuring performance. It is essential to involve the appraisee in drawing up the plans so that there is and agreed basis of commitment.

Readers familiar with force-field analysis know how useful it is to identify the forces assisting and resisting any change, and to plan to maximise the one and minimise the other. Also useful will be the SWOT analysis (see page 157), and the problem-solving methods mentioned above. Any complex objective will need to be broken into stages, or 'stepping stones'.

7. Coaching

We take the view that the individual's training and development is the joint responsibility of the manager and the individual – with the individuals taking responsibility for their own learning and the manager acting as sponsor, guide and support. The manager can be a coach, that is someone committed to the trainee's progress and development who can give objective feedback and who can offer controlled delegation of tasks. The good coach helps someone to learn in a variety of ways, and provides opportunities for practice in a safe setting.

There are good reasons why this role falls ideally, but not always, to the line manager. It is traditionally a rewarding part of the boss/manager relationship, and like delegation, can be integrated into the appraisal process. One must bear in mind the dangers of either being over-protective or leaving the individual to sink or swim. A good coach will:

- identify the individual's strengths and weaknesses;
- develop trust;
- create a structured plan for development;
- identify the blocks to successful performance;
- be a good listener – available to the individual, if necessary, physically, intellectually and emotionally;
- understand the individual's effective learning style;
- link coaching to delegated tasks;
- be supportive but not afraid to challenge.

Learning Sets
There is a good case for developing coaching by peers and for using learning sets to support individuals. This method involves groups of individuals meeting regularly with a facilitator to identify and support individual learning objectives for everyone in the group.

8. Delegation

Achievement never comes without delegation. It is implicit in any organisational structure. Managers who fail to delegate end up overworked and very likely caught in the crisis-management mode where all problems become critical before they are dealt with. The second reason for delegation is that it is one of the best ways to develop staff.

Delegation is the *planned* assignment to subordinates of responsibility for carrying out work, together with the necessary authority and resources that go with it. It is not simply instructing people or giving them short-term assignments that need the manager's approval for any decisions. Delegation is most effective when the person is given a lot of control over what he or she can do – but it can be progressive, with larger and larger amounts of work delegated as the individual develops confidence and competence (and the manager is more confident to entrust the individual with it). Delegation should involve a time frame, progress reviews and some kind of debriefing.

Delegation is easier where the work chosen is not too critical or demanding; it should be self-contained and achievable within a reasonable time scale. There must be enough time to do the necessary planning, coaching and follow up. Other considerations include the experienced supervision available and the individual's existing experience and understanding. Ideally, the task should be one where any mistakes are retrievable, and where there are no professional restrictions to delegation. It is best if it forms part of a planned programme of staff development. Do not offer assorted administrative trivia which you as a manager find boring. The individual should be receptive to advice and correction. More experienced staff should not feel deprived or frustrated as a result.

One of the dilemmas about delegation is that people realise that it is useful only when they are under too much pressure to be able to do it! The appraisal discussion provides an ideal opportunity to discuss delegation, and this links the setting of objectives with personal development planning.

In Chapter 2 we mentioned the restrictions on delegation as part of a traditional professional culture (the 'bleep culture') that can prevent change and staff development.

'I get job satisfaction from doing this – I dislike the idea of delegating it.'

'The doctors like to know that I do this personally – they may lose confidence if someone junior does it.'

'What if the person makes a mess of it? It could be embarrassing.'

'It will take too much time to explain everything.'

Any manager will need to take account of these feelings and find ways of getting round them. All too often in the past people's development has been thwarted by fears about delegation. Remember that people will never get the chance to be really useful if they are never given the chance to show what they are capable of.

How to Delegate

Delegation is not an all-or-nothing decision. The level of delegation can expand: close supervision at first is followed by a gradual release of controls until the member of staff takes over completely. The steps might be as follows.

- *Describe the task*
  Explain why the task is necessary and the outcome wanted.
  Highlight significant things that might occur and explain how to respond.
  Discuss and confirm the responsibility and authority required.
  Summarise the requirements and check they are understood.
- *Monitor delegation*
  Ask for a report back.

Be available for emergencies.
Review the assignment and debrief fully.
- *Extend delegation gradually*
Let the trainee tell you what he or she will do.
Extend the complexity of the task.
Provide less and less direct supervision.
Allow the person to tackle increasingly difficult problems.
Extend scope for decision making.

9. Giving Feedback

Reviews

Conducting reviews calls for specific skills and comes much more naturally to some managers than others. Reviews should not only take place within the framework of the formal appraisal situation. Consider the many other opportunities:

- daily or weekly informal progress review (eg, ward handover);
- bimonthly performance or goal achievement reviews;
- probationary period review;
- on completion of a work cycle or assignment (eg, pathology laboratory bench rotations);
- after undertaking a training event;
- when performance has been exceptional;
- when performance declines or something goes wrong;
- when taking over supervision a new group of staff;
- prior to transfer or termination of employment;
- after mergers, reorganisations or other significant changes.

The purposes may be concerned with performance assessment, achievement of objectives, learning and personal development, morale, work allocation, team building, grievances, project evaluation, handovers of work, redeployment, etc. The skills required are basically the same. Above all, make sure that reviews are seen as time for the individual, where their needs can have priority, rather than some kind of disciplinary correction session that meets your needs rather than theirs.

Guidelines for Giving Feedback

Make it clear, factual and related to specific behaviour. Balance praise and criticism – mention strengths and weaknesses, and do not overdo the criticism. Give it as early as possible. Use confirmatory evidence – including others' judgement. Above all, encourage self-assessment and participation and the recognition of development needs.

An example of unsound feedback is: 'Your case management has been quite good but you could have tried a bit harder in some areas and been a bit more professional sometimes'. Whereas sound feedback would be: 'Your case management this year has demonstrated sensitivity to patient needs, excellent coordination with others and intelligent application of your clinical knowledge. However, your reports have not quite been up to the standard required. They were often too short, and lacked sufficient detail. Were you aware of this? Why do you think it is?'

The first is vague, unhelpful and over-judgemental. It is likely to lead to misunderstanding or resentment. The second is specific and encouraging. It invites open constructive discussion and leads to an agreed development plan.

Correction
'Correction' and 'criticism' have connotations of adverse judgements and even punishment. In our context, self-correction is the obvious ideal. This is more likely to come about where the person has set their own goals from the start. There are many situations when the manager will be expected by the subordinate to provide corrective information. If the manager needs to point out deficiencies it should be prompt, private and specific. Reasons for the correction should be given, and criticism should be of the behaviour rather than the person. Make reference to agreed standards or procedures where possible, and encourage the individual to develop their own correction plan. Avoid being accusatory, judgemental or vindictive. Do not be manipulative, condescending, belittling or patronising, either. Offer continuing advice, support, training and monitoring when required.

On Being Appraised

Many of the skills mentioned above may be required by the appraisee as well as the appraiser. When considering your own appraisal with your boss, remember that you will not be able to set objectives for others if your own direction is not clear. Give thought to your role and aspirations before the meeting. Make your boss aware of your aims and capability, and push for clarification, action, commitment. Be ready to accept challenges, but do not accept any deal that you do not have the capability to deliver, or where you feel the price paid is too high. Be assertive when necessary and constructive where possible.

Summary

The appraiser's three key roles are to *sponsor*, *monitor* and *support*. The sponsor role is about creating the working contract in the first place, reinforcing it and adapting it. The monitor role involves review, assessment and correction, judging and deciding the quality of people's work contributions and remedies for shortfalls. The support role promotes individual staff interests.

The nine key competences for conducting appraisals are:

1. Listening
2. Interviewing
3. Assessment
4. Influencing
5. Problem solving
6. Performance planning
7. Coaching
8. Delegation
9. Giving feedback.

If it is necessary, *correction* should be prompt, private and specific. A good manager will encourage the individual to develop their own correction plan.

Chapter 7

Who Will Call the Tune? Setting Standards and Objectives

This chapter explains the principles involved in setting standards and objectives, which are necessary to appraise staff and make useful measurements of their performance. Removing any trepidation the manager may feel about these issues will enable us later (Chapter 8) to develop objectives to reflect the wider demands of the organisation and work roles.

Objectives and standards are forged by agreement during a formal appraisal process. If we try to set objectives unilaterally outside this process we may fail to take account of legitimate staff expectations or align our expectations with theirs. In addition, individuals may not feel the same accountability for results and important aspects of staff development may be neglected.

Defining Standards

It is not compulsory to use objectives in performance appraisal. It is possible to use standards, which can be based on measures of work quality or output, competences, or specially developed ratings of performance. Standards are measurable criteria or indicators of level of performance. They normally specify a behaviour, output requirements or outcome to be achieved as an indication of meeting the standard.

If the task were making tea, then we might set the following standards.

Filling the kettle safely.
Checking the requirements of consumers for milk and sugar.

Achieving a liquid strength within defined concentrations.
Getting satisfactory comments from consumers.
Ensuring the kitchen is left tidy and clean.

Note that each of these is assessable, although to ensure consistent assessment we may need to refine our criteria. For example, describe safe (and perhaps dangerous) practice for filling a kettle. How is the liquid strength to be measured – scientifically, or by subjective judgement (eg, tasting it)? Do we need a visual guide to assessing tea strength? How will we get the customers' reaction, ensuring they do not suppress complaints out of politeness or gratitude? What does 'satisfactory' mean? How do we measure tidiness – what are the criteria? Must all crockery be put away? Each of these is independent of the others, although we could set standards that are linked in some way; for example, the first might need to be reached before the second could be achieved.

Why Set Standards?
- They identify requirements.
- They provide a basis for training and instruction.
- They help focus tasks and activities.
- They ensure consistent of activity and behaviour.
- They help motivate people to achieve.

Defining Objectives
Objectives, on the other hand, involve reaching a goal or achieving some result, to a given standard, in a given time period, within defined constraints and resources. For example, the objective might be: 'To provide a cup of tea for five people to their requirements before 5pm using the provisions and equipment provided'. Here we have: an achievement and standard (to provide a cup of tea for five people to their requirements); a reference to time (before 5pm); a reference to other resources (using the provisions and equipment provided).

All objectives can be reduced to a very simple formula:

To achieve a certain result
to a certain standard
within a stated time period.

We usually need to add details of what resources are available and define the standard or result to be obtained (*a performance criterion*). We may need to specify, or qualify, how the result is to be obtained (*action plan*) and measured.

There is no need to set an objective when a standard will do just as well. We can use standards alone where we are talking about situations where the outcome is straightforward, and can be achieved quickly, without consideration of resource use or planning for implementation

Why Set Objectives?

Objectives are a basis for focusing effort, providing motivation and identifying key outcomes. Setting objectives can provide the means of clarifying work requirements and responsibilities. They assist us in planning changes and thus help establish control over activities and provide the basis for monitoring performance and progress. Besides all this, reaching objectives gives people a sense of achievement.

Are Objectives Always Necessary?

Setting objectives lends itself to situations where results can be defined over a period of time. For instance, in staff performance review and appraisal, where they can be the basis of a clearly defined contract with the member of staff or team. Objectives help us plan changes and projects, services and budgets, and individual plans for patient care or staff development. Note the need to have clear-cut results (*outcomes*) and time scales. It is difficult or inappropriate to set objectives where there is disagreement about desired outcomes, where a situation is very fluid or uncontrollable, or when it is impossible to make objective measurements.

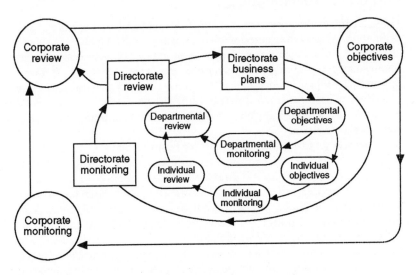

Figure 7.1 A 'top down' model of linked performance cycles

Objective setting also tends to fail where a situation is very complex, or when there are too many objectives to be manageable. The complex arrangement shown in Figure 7.1 may look good on the chief executive's desk, but in practice is unmanageable unless confined to one or two key results, such as reduction of waiting times, or achievement of budgets. The problem with such grand schemes is that they are often experienced as remote constraints that remove individual control and stifle initiative. Too often in the past, there has been a failure to link corporate objectives with the work done by individuals. Nevertheless, performance management allied to business planning at directorate level can help integrate the different levels of objectives and relate them to jobs and required standards.

Objectives Derive from Expectations

Before we look at objective setting in detail we need to explore the expectations from which they derive. Managers need to respond to four sources of expectations: *corporate expectations*; *service expectations*; *staff expectations*; and *professional expectations*.

Corporate Expectations

These are the expectations of senior management and are the basis of any evaluation of the performance of the organisation and its managers. These are likely to include strategic objectives, based on achieving output and financial targets, but may well include targets for quality and staff development as well. It is very likely that some (not all) general corporate objectives will be cascaded down to form directorate and departmental objectives, each time indicating the concrete contributions required at each level (see Figure 7.1).

These will set goals and constraints for business plans. Goals are likely to involve targets on an organisation-wide basis and refer to output or activity levels, budget limits, time scales for completion of projects or delivery of services, or prevention of adverse incidents. Such targets may be agreed by the board, and will not therefore be negotiable by department managers – although the contributions made by individual departments, or the time span of introduction or completion may be. They will impact on the manager at service department level in a number of ways. The corporate or departmental objectives will have a major influence on departmental goals and hence on team and individual objectives.

The Impact of Corporate Strategies

Typically the organisation will develop a series of strategies, including, for instance: revenue planning; capital planning and return on investment; corporate planning and service development; contract achievement; service quality; human resources; customer care and complaints; risk management; health and safety; information; communications; marketing; professional training and development; and joint strategies agreed with other organisations (like Social Services or Purchasing Authorities).

The healthcare manager setting objectives at departmental level will need to consider the impact these strategies have on the setting of departmental goals and business plans. They may impose specific goals at directorate and departmental level or create objectives for certain individuals. The manager may also need to ask whether any resources will be made available (or taken away) – if so where will they be found, and how are they negotiated for? On the positive side, a particular corporate strategy may provide opportunities for selective developments of people or services. It may usefully put a spotlight on the department. Other strategies may be more general – here one may want to influence interpretation to ensure local needs are addressed. Business planning (see Appendix) is a process for enabling directorates or departments to plan their priorities in the light of corporate objectives.

Opportunities Arising from Corporate Strategies

Here are some typical examples of opportunites for service improvements and staff development which arose from the demands of meeting particular corporate strategies. In all cases they provided worthwhile objectives for particular staff.

The unit strategy for *customer care and complaints* required a customer care survey to be carried out by directorates, with help from management consultants, who helped directorates build a database (used for raising staff awareness and monitoring progress). Some staff were involved in project teams with objectives to conduct surveys and follow up areas where improvements were needed.

A corporate *revenue planning* strategy required the planned devolution of budgets. This was implemented by finance staff in an agreed sequence, directorate by directorate. Someone was charged with planning the implementation in the department. The result was better local control of resources and the opportunity for some staff training in this area.

A *professional development* strategy devolved funding for professional development to directorates, where business plans were required to include a local professional development plan. This enabled staff and service development to be linked and resourced accurately, and was a spur to the creation of development plans for each member of staff. Implementation was a key objective for some managerial staff.

A revised *discharge policy* was agreed as a result of discussions with other local care organisations. In each directorate practice was reviewed by designated staff. Their investigations and suggestions led to an improvement in practice and a clarification of roles.

Service Expectations

A second important set of expectations concern meeting day-to-day operational demands to provide services. The aim is to make the best possible use of resources to provide a given standard of care, and to maintain its continuity despite largely unpredictable pressures.

The activities required to keep essential services going tend to be at the level of fighting the alligators, when draining the swamp may be the corporate goal. In a hospital there is an expectation that patients will be seen, admitted, found beds, treated, tested, discharged, supplied with drugs and generally looked after: in other words we are talking about managing the essential workload. Managers and staff need to exercise energy and ingenuity in making sure that things keep going. It typically involves keeping up the levels of productivity, solving operational problems, eking out meagre resources, removing blockages, developing people – and keeping them going.

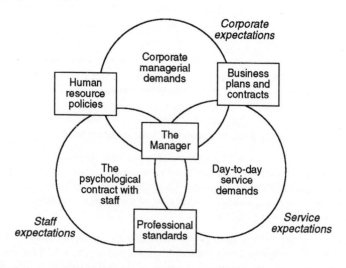

Figure 7.2 The manager holds the ring between different expectations

Staff Expectations

A third source of expectations come from the staff themselves, who will have needs and aspirations, both individually and collectively. Meeting staff expectations will involve responding to their needs and developing them, as well as maintaining motivation. Neglecting such staff expectations will lead to frustration, demotivation, a loss of initiatives and skills, and a loss of the good will on which the service often depends. Chronically high levels of turnover, stress and sickness absence tend to result when staff needs are neglected. Less obvious effects are poor standards of care resulting from a decline of interest in work, or from a neglect of training. Organisations must foster staff loyalty – uncertainty and threats of redundancy undermine commitment and confidence. In addition, places where staff are treated badly get bad reputations and this drives away recruits.

An important consequence of pressure on the staffing resource is the lack of time for staff to work free from patient contact or service demands. Such time is often regarded as totally dispensable if patient demand calls for it – both in planning staffing levels and in day-to-day operation. Yet such time to reflect and plan is essential for staff and organisation development.

Professional Expectations

Professional expectations operate across organisations somewhat independently of the particular management process and are governed both by statute and by the requirements of professional bodies. In the concern for achieving business goals and coping with day-to-day pressures, concern is often expressed that standards are at risk and that nationally recommended levels of practice and training are being neglected. The professional leadership role a manager carries may not always synchronise with the demands of managerial accountability.

Setting Priorities

These sets of expectations interact and are sometimes in conflict. They call for decisions of priority. They may all get raised to a level of insistent demands where the manager – charged with holding the ring between them – finds it hard to cope.

The setting of objectives to meet so many different expectations seems daunting. Should every expectation be made into an objective? If so, the list will probably be overwhelming. How do we balance staff development with the need to achieve targets within the directorate, for example? Does every member of staff need to have a long list of objectives to work on? It may be that some staff are happier with having to achieve standards than objectives. Who has which objectives? Do staff have a say, or are objectives imposed? Imposition is demotivating, yet negotiation might appear to be exhausting and time consuming. How does one keep track of them all? Do they all need to be measured? It all starts to look like a nightmare of supervision and paperwork.

The feeling of being straitjacketed by objectives, and the bureaucracy that goes with them, has led in the past to a rejection of complicated systems of management by objectives in many organisations. It has even led managers to shy away from carrying out appraisals and staff to become confused and overwhelmed. So we must not allow anyone to get carried away by the idea of objective setting. The reader may feel disheartened at this point. Can objective setting, which seems so useful, *really* become a manager's nightmare?

The answer is to limit this objective-setting process, to ensure that it can work, that we retain control of it, and that staff are happy with the demands made by it – to ensure that setting objectives actually improves performance in the end. This may mean managers resisting those people who may want to push your objectives setting too far, especially when it is new. Here are some possible ways of containing and prioritising objectives.

1. Set Objectives for What Matters Most
It is possible to limit objectives to certain themes. For instance, if there is pressure on you to achieve certain activity levels or savings, everyone could have objectives that relate to that broad aim. It should stimulate teamwork – but it may be that other key areas get neglected.

2. Set Objectives for What you and your Staff can Cope with
This makes sense, but has its dangers: objectives may not be taken seriously, or be set too low. The manager may need to ensure that priorities are addressed, and ensure that targets are met even though they may not feature as anyone's objectives.

3. Set Broad Team or Departmental Objectives and Allow Scope for Individual Contributions
It can be useful to set out what is demanded from the department (for example, business plan targets) and allow staff to say how they will contribute to their achievement, without being too prescriptive about it. If this has an element of risk, the extra motivation of staff is likely to compensate for it – provided the manager can guide the choice of outcomes.

4. Use a Team-building Session to Generate Objectives that Integrate Service Priorities and Individual Needs and Aspirations

An 'awayday' or team-building session is used to identify collectively where the department or team is at present, where it should be going, and who will take responsibility for particular agreed objectives (see Appendix 2, page 159). It requires a lot of time and work – for instance, in collecting information, planning the day, facilitating the discussions, leading staff and gaining commitment from them to changes and improved performance. On the other hand, staff get a lot from it, and it can generate a great deal of energy and motivation. It is important that scope is given for putting the ideas into practice afterwards or the whole thing may backfire, particularly if over-ambitious projects have been agreed.

5. Work up Objectives that Develop People's Current Jobs

This is based on identifying key result areas for each individual, and offers the chance to update job descriptions, so it fits in well with many appraisal schemes. It may result in objectives that are relatively small scale, unexciting or ignore team contributions.

6. Concentrate on Staff Development

A strong culture of continuous development can result in high levels of performance. For this to work, the manager must link development shrewdly to the achievement of service needs, developing a vision of future requirements as well as of current needs.

7. Leave some Staff out of the Process of Direct Objective Setting Altogether – or Extend it Gradually through the Staff Group

We might consider excluding staff whose work does not lend itself to having objectives set. For them, standards of output or of competence may be more useful. The obvious danger is the creation of two classes of worker – those who have objectives and those who do not. Such considerations may suggest a sequential introduction of appraisal (see Chapter 5), where the process is extended gradually to everyone, being allowed to settled down adequately within each group in turn.

The strategy you choose will depend on your own situation – how confident you feel, as well as what the staff are likely to be able to handle, and what demands the organisation is making on you for results, following from the performance appraisal scheme or as a result of general pressures on managers. We need to make sure that when we set objectives, we do it realistically.

Characteristics of Good Objectives

Objectives must refer to *important results* for a department or individual. For performance objectives, consider the relationship between the manager's and department objectives and the key tasks or result areas of the individual's job. Vague, ambiguous objectives are useless. They must be *specific*. They must be *achievable* yet should also be *challenging*. It must be possible to assess the degree to which objectives have been achieved, so they must be *assessable*. It is important that objectives are *agreed* so people feel some ownership of their objective – at the very least, having control over how the objective is to be reached (the action plan), even if the objective itself is predetermined. An agreed objective is a kind of contract.

Other Important Requirements

The manager (or other sponsor) is concerned with providing *support and training*. People must be given the *authority*, that is, the legitimate power to make things happen.

Setting objectives requires that some kind of *review* is built into the process. That review is agreed at the start, and first happens well before the completion date. It is used to identify progress made, to offer help with problems, and to assist or people whose performance may be falling below requirements. When setting objectives, the *resources* needed must be considered. Besides resources like finance and time, the manager should consider less obvious but equally important kinds, like authority (to take decisions), information and cooperation. Managers need to ensure that objectives remain flexible and can be changed when conditions or resource levels change.

There should be a *target time* set for the start and completion of each objective, which can be adjusted if necessary. Action plans will often contain definite 'milestones', the stepping stones by which the individual reaches the goal, with more detail being added later on. Some objectives take a short time to complete, others a whole year. At an agreed time a final review takes place. Consider the control the individual has as well as the pressures on the manager and other staff. It will not be satisfactory at the end of the year to say 'we did not get round to it'.

Objectives should *motivate* staff. This will not happen if they are a restatement of job descriptions, a list of job constraints, or a restatement of the manager's objectives with action plans attached. It is better to set objectives that release the imagination of individuals to develop schemes that meet service objectives in a cost effective way.

It becomes difficult to track more than about six objectives. Therefore there is a need to *limit* objectives or combine related objectives under one heading.

What to Record

The following should be recorded:

- the objective
- the required outcome – with details of how it will be measured or assessed
- the resources that will be provided
- the support, training and authority that will be provided by the sponsoring manager
- any agreed action plan.

The appraisee agrees to undertake the necessary training, which must be sufficient to provide the necessary competences to achieve the results required.

Different kinds of objective include:

- *departmental or team objective*, concerned with desired changes, or project planning, where often the whole team is involved;
- *individual performance objective*, where one individual has to achieve some agreed result;
- *individual development objective*, where the agreed result involves personal development such as learning a new competence;

Objectives also involve *innovation, improvement* and *maintenance* – to establish (or set up), improve (the operation of), and maintain (keep going) to certain standards. If there is little growth, yet effort and resourcefulness are required to maintain essential services or to cope with difficult conditions, maintenance objectives are important.

Objectives may relate to activity, quality, use of resources (including finance and information), procedures and communications, or to the development of staff.

Performance objectives should identify results required, and relate these to those planned for the department. Similarly, the result required for *development objectives* will be something reflecting that individual's development. They can form part of a personal development plan (see Chapter 9). Performance and development objectives will often coincide.

Performance objectives (or *task standards*) must be derived from important aspects of the person's work role. Besides the job description, they can also come from team contributions, projects and assignments (see Chapter 8). This can be useful when work roles are changing.

Cascading objectives are where one person's objectives are linked to another person's. Managers will want to ensure that the order in which objectives are set allows delegation of work to take place in a rational way.

Controlling One's Own Objectives as a Manager

Many managers are now faced with unprecedented demands, and expectations that they feel unable to meet. Far from being empowered, they feel immobilised. You should be positive yet shrewd when establishing your own objectives. Be clear about what is required by when, and what resources are being made available. Be proactive in your discussion of priorities and resources. Show willing, but identify and agree what is *realistic*. Don't be negative on the one hand, or too 'gung ho' on the other. Allow for unforeseen circumstances – discuss contingencies. Ensure there is sufficient balance between different demands. Point out any contradictions between priorities. Ensure there is scope for your staff to adapt and undertake development programmes (and for you to do so, too!).

Summary

Standards are measurable criteria or indicators of level of performance. They normally specify a behaviour, output requirements or outcome to be achieved as an indication of meeting the standard. Setting standards helps to identify requirements, provides a basis for training and instruction, focuses tasks and activities, ensures consistent of activity and behaviour and motivates people to achieve.

Objectives involve reaching a goal or achieving some result in a given time and to a given standard, within defined constraints and resources – they must be specific, achievable and assessable. A statement of objectives should include what resources are available for use and the standard or result to be obtained (a performance criterion). Objectives help in focusing effort, providing motivation, identifying key outcomes and can be used to clarify work requirements and responsibilities. They assist us in planning changes and thus help establish control over activities, monitor performance and progress, and give people a sense of achievement.

Objectives derive from corporate, service, staff or professional expectations. A set of objectives can constitute a personal achievement plan, containing objectives for both performance and development, which may coincide.

Chapter 8

Objectives and Jobs

This chapter is concerned with getting clear what people in the team are required to do. People are sometimes heard to say, with genuine concern: 'There's my job – and then there are my objectives – they do not seem to relate to each other!'

We need to ensure that there are links between job and objectives, otherwise we can end up with a free-for-all where objectives are distributed arbitrarily (and often inappropriately) to members of the work team, or objective-setting becomes a substitute for job definition, so people have long lists of tasks set out as objectives, rather than a proper job description.

At this stage we are again looking at the creation of objectives separately from the interactive processes involved in appraisal and review, in order to get the specification right. In practice this emerges interactively during appraisal and performance review, as described in Chapter 5.

To get a clear idea of work roles, we must start by looking at the traditional job description.

Job Descriptions

Are Job Descriptions of Any Use?

The value of job descriptions has often been questioned. Serious mismatches occur between what a *person* thinks they do, what the *manager* thinks they do, and what they *actually* do. And none of these may look anything like the document in the personnel files called the job description which was sent out with the recruitment literature years ago when the job was advertised. That is only fished out when someone demands a regrading or when they are in disciplinary trouble.

Standard job descriptions are usually poor at stating objectives clearly enough to enable performance to be measured directly. They often fail to identify short-term assignments and projects, and they omit process requirements (how the job-holder performs). Many fail to describe required competences accurately and ignore team contributions. They need frequent updating as requirements and conditions change. These limitations make it a poor instrument for performance assessment, or for identifying development needs in relation to the job.

Yet we have to work with job descriptions, with all their limitations, if we are concerned with the management of performance. Questions about the style, content and effectiveness of job descriptions are likely to be addressed to the personnel department, who are seen as the owners. This is a pity since it is a management tool of vital importance to all who manage people. There is a good case, then, for making job descriptions work for you, and using them as the starting point for describing and assessing performance requirements. You may want to improve them, and I offer some suggestions for doing this (by creating what I call a 'work role statement') later on.

There is usually an organisational 'house style' for job descriptions. Managers are usually asked to provide the first draft and agree the final content. You may well find that your organisation uses a format for job descriptions with headings like those shown in Figure 8.1.

JOB DESCRIPTION PART I

- Title/Department/Grade/Hours
- Accountable to/Responsible to
- Job Purpose Statement
- Key Result Areas or Main Areas of Responsibility
- Dimensions of Job*
- Communications and Working Relationships
- Competences Required
- Qualifications and Experience Necessary
- Organisation Chart

* *Dimensions* provide the size indicators that are useful for grading. They include details of the throughput, staffing and budgets for which the person is responsible – useful when comparing jobs or clarifying accountability for resources.

Figure 8.1 Format heading for job description

The Purpose of Job Descriptions

The main purpose of job descriptions is to indicate accountabilities – to whom and for what; to specify overall job purpose; and to specify particular standing or ongoing responsibilities. The document can then be used for assigning grading, clarifying responsibilities, writing person specifications (for recruitment) and determining training needs, as well as identifying performance requirements.

'Accountable to...' and 'responsible to...' are sometimes separately identified since the person with day-to-day supervisory responsibility may not be the person who 'hires and fires'.

It is useful to have a job purpose statement at the beginning, as objectives and standards of performance will derive from it. However, this is not usually adequate to enable a complete picture of all the performance requirements to be drawn up.

Job descriptions usually state standing responsibilities either in terms of key result areas (often also called 'principal accountabilities'), or, alternatively, as 'key tasks' (some hybrid versions also exist). There is an important difference between these ways of describing responsibilities, and some dispute about which is the best format. Let me illustrate the difference by using the work of a hospital car park attendant as an example. Two key responsibilities might involve directing traffic to the right areas and collecting and banking payments.

The more traditional format (using *key tasks*) might put this as follows:

To direct traffic to designated parking areas.
To redirect drivers whose cars are parked incorrectly.
To contact motorists via hospital tannoy system when required.
To clamp vehicle wheels when necessary.
To empty cash machine.
To bank cash with general office.
To observe financial and security requirements.

This form is detailed, rather long-winded and lends itself to the setting of standards rather than objectives – for example, you can set standards of efficiency, courtesy or timeliness for many of these tasks.

However, using a *key result areas* format, it might look different:

To ensure all cars are parked safely and appropriately according to parking policy.
To ensure payments are obtained and banked with minimum risk in line with hospital requirements.

This is not mere semantic twiddling. Using this format stresses *results required* rather than *tasks*, and suggests that there may be a number of ways of achieving these results. The person might be allowed to use their initiative. Without changing the wording, we can embrace current priorities, like preventing cars parking on grassed areas if we see that as a fairly specific current short-term objective. If critics argue that the 'ensure...' type statements are too vague, we can spell out sub-objectives to the extent we want to, but again, we must state them in terms of results.

I think the key results format is more useful when we want to define performance in terms of results or outcomes (and therefore when objectives rather than standards are to be set). I do accept, however, that some very simple jobs may not suit this format. The choice of format will depend to some extent on the scope the individual has for determining *how* results are achieved (which relates to the level of skill required in the job) and on how the job performance is to be monitored (close or distant supervision, short- or long-term assessment). It will also determine the kinds of performance objectives set (see Chapter 7). Whichever format is chosen it is helpful to split this into not more than seven main areas, with subheadings specifying more detailed responsibilities.

How to Describe Responsibilities as Key Result Areas

Start each statement with a verb, as active as possible. The useful verbs are those that are concrete and which indicate results that can be assessed, such as *ensure, make certain, complete, determine, maintain, record, report, monitor, evaluate. Ensure* is particularly useful as it automatically specifies a result or outcome. Less good are *liaise with, assist with, care for, initiate, provide, co-ordinate, service, facilitate.* The word *manage* can be ambiguous unless you spell out the precise meaning in subheadings. If you are going to use words like coordinate, try to specify measurable results of *coordination* (see example 2 below).

Do not make the sentences too long (say more than 12 words). Do not put in unrelated details just for the sake of completeness: you will never cover everything, in any case.

Example I

To ensure that *patient records* are maintained *according to requirements.*

(Active verb)   (Noun)   (Qualifying phrase)

Example 2

To coordinate the professional team in order to ensure

1. effective assessment takes place within five days of arrival
2. joint care plans are drawn up
3. discharge summaries are agreed by the whole clinical team.

Because we are interested in *performance*, it makes sense to write job descriptions in such a way that it is possible to assess whether or not the result has been achieved or the task carried out satisfactorily. Statements in job descriptions that fail to specify results, such as:

to be responsible for patient care
to have concern for the safety of patients and staff
to liaise over discharges

are of little value as statements of tasks or key result areas, although they may be used as riders to other, more meaningful statements, indicating values and priorities, for example:

To carry out initial assessments of patients discharged from hospital care, first ensuring that required discharge procedures have been carried out satisfactorily.
To identify and implement wheelchair maintenance requirements ensuring priority is given to all aspects of patient safety.

If you have clarity about departmental objectives, the next stage is to determine how these goals will be achieved by the staff available. They need to fit in with existing job descriptions, which might require amendment. Whether or not you want to review in detail the job descriptions of all the staff who report to you as a manager, you might find it useful to consider the key result areas each staff member has responsibility for. Are they clear, and appropriate? Do they lend themselves to developing individual objectives in a flexible way? Do some staff have jobs (or ability levels) to which clearly defined tasks and standards are more appropriate?

Then consider what has to be currently achieved, in terms of results and standards. Can you relate these into key result areas for staff? Do your job descriptions relate to the department or team objectives, or must you think about changing peoples roles significantly? You may find it hard to assign things to individuals, where team objectives seem more appropriate. Team and project briefings need to be created where necessary.

Work Role Statements

It is useful to use the term 'work role statement' to describe the contribution of an individual, which will involve some or all of the following:

- key result areas
- key tasks
- required competences
- projects and assignments, and
- required team contributions.

We can make this work role statement into a reference document which lists all the contributions which the individual is expected to make in their work for the period in question. It can be as detailed as you want it. It is a more current and useful version of the job description, since it also details assignments and team membership. Changes are agreed with the manager at the appraisal meeting.

We can set priorities in terms of key objectives for that individual within their agreed work role in any of the above areas, or we can assign standards to tasks. The key objectives or standards will be stated in the Part II document shown in Figure 8.2 (Part I will be the job description shown in Figure 8.1), and can be reviewed during performance review and appraisal.

Figure 8.2 Job description, Part II

Part II Job Information Update/Short Term Commitments

Changes in job responsibilities
This updates the job description. Indicate any changes in key result areas.

Current assignments, projects and secondments
Please indicate any changes since the last review, including responsibilities for meeting project objectives.

Current team contributions
Indicate any changes since the last review, including responsibilities for meeting team objectives.

Current objectives (or standards required).
Include both performance and developmental objectives, stating results.

(The job description may state tasks and duties rather than key result areas.)

Many people now consider it useful to refer to competences, particularly for jobs such as that of healthcare assistant. Normally there are competence standards that can be assessed. The reference standards may be at threshold level or at a higher standard, and we thus can build in some individual developmental objectives by using this standard. There is a link between the required competences and the individual's personal development plan.

Assignments and projects may be of short-term duration, and are rarely included in explicit detail in standard job descriptions. However, they are indispensable in delegating responsibility for the achievement of goals, and for developing staff. They need to be recorded in any work role definition. So also do team contributions. This is to recognise the fact that much work is achieved through teamwork. Most healthcare managers will see this component as vital, although rarely is it formally assessed or even mentioned in personnel documents.

The work required under each of the above components may have some formal accountability attached to it. It will be useful to identify contributions people make, even though formal accountability is held by someone else.

Work roles can be expressed in a number of ways, for instance in terms of key result areas alone, or assignments alone, or competences – or any combination of these things. To use these statements for the management of performance it is important to ensure that appropriate results and standards are attached to each component (see the example, below). This may refer to what is achieved (result) or the way in which it is achieved (process).

Key result area (from job description):
To ensure supplies costs are kept within budget.

Key objective (1), derived from key result area:
To ensure supplies costs are kept within budget for period 1995/6.

Key objective (2), derived from key result area:
To develop zero based budget (by ...) to provide the basis for accurate monthly monitoring of supplies costs.

We can derive key objectives in the same way from team contributions or project roles, for example:

Project involvement:
Member of waiting list initiative project team.

Key objective:
To design and implement recommended new procedures in department by 1.1.96.

Where the job content is described in terms of tasks, key standards can be set instead of objectives:

Task (from job description):
To ensure supplies are ordered promptly and that overstocking is avoided.

Example of key standard derived from task standard:
To ensure all supplies requested are available within five working days and that stock levels remain within agreed target levels.

These work role statements describe all the activities required from an individual worker. Although they incorporate the content of an accurate, current job description, they go beyond this by defining the results and standards required.

They are specific to one particular worker, not general job templates. They can describe competences, assignments and the person's team role and refer to that particular worker's development needs. In addition, they allow for fairly easy updating

Giving People the Authority they Need

Whether we are talking about standing responsibilities in the traditional job description, or other components of the work role, we need to allow the person some scope to make decisions, commensurate with the size of the responsibility delegated, and in their manager's absence. This is sometimes neglected in health service jobs: the 'bleep culture' inhibits delegation of authority and therefore empowerment. Staff must not be criticised unfairly for using their authority in a reasonable way, even if the results are sometimes not perfect. As a manager you need to ensure that your own authority is adequate, especially before delegating responsibilities.

For such delegation to work, it must be clear to all concerned that this person has full responsibility in this area and reports to the manager. The person must have sufficient authority to resolve difficulties, to call on resources and be assured cooperation from others. The person's manager may however be called upon to intervene supportively when required (this should not be often, or the individual's credibility will be lost).

So, the manager must prepare the ground by briefing whoever needs to know, and ensuring where necessary that resources are designated. Delegation may however be done in stages (see pages 96–98).

A clear-cut sense of accountability and authority should always be the aim, but this will be diminished where there is inadequate definition, sponsorship from the manager, or control over results in practice (see Crosby, 1992). For instance, the accountability may be qualified by unspecific words like 'contribute to', 'liaise with', or only vague joint accountability is specified. Accountability may be given for operating procedures rather than achieving results. Sometimes the stated job accountability is clearly false because others possess the authority to remove resources or override decisions, or the manager backs down when the subordinate's decision is challenged. Sometimes new working arrangements (such as task groups, projects, committees or, 'matrix management') are set up which confuse accountability and do not specify who has authority to take decisions. Crosby reminds us that accountabilities must be determined in conjunction with those who can affect results.

Problems with Accountability and Authority

1. In a general hospital, a bed manager role is introduced on a fairly junior grade, with the person given accountability for ensuring bed availability. Medical consultants currently make decisions about discharges and admissions.
    Can the job be done?
2. A reduction in staff absenteeism is set as an objective.
    Should the line manager or personnel manager be accountable for results?
3. Clerks are required to ensure accurate return of information on patient status. The accuracy of the figures depends on professional staff completing the returns assiduously.
    Is it fair to set standards of accuracy for the ward clerk' s work?
4. A therapy services manager finds that in trying to achieve her 'key result' of improving communications with GPs she is in competition with a group set up on a Trust wide basis to make recommendations for improvements. GPs complain to the chief executive that they are getting too many people asking for information about services.
    The therapy services manager is asked to refrain from taking any action.

Comments:

1. The bed manager either needs to be given the authority to overrule consultants' decisions if necessary (unlikely!), or her accountability must allow for the latter. It could be to maximise available bed use, it might involve some responsibility to talk to consultants and persuade them to release beds, by individual negotiation and agreement, or through some sort of bed use arbitration committee. It may be within

the bed manager's role to devise such mechanisms, or to ensure that the procedures already set up were operated.

2. The personnel manager and line managers contribute to the achievement of the result. It may be reasonable to make the personnel manager accountable for ensuring that appropriate procedures are in place and are effective, and even that managers are persuaded to act as required. The line manager may feel that the particular sickness problems in her department are intractable ones, and if she is to be made accountable for results here, they need to be carefully stated.

3. It is likely that the clerks can achieve the standards required provided the exercise is supported strongly managerially. There may need to be sanctions on professionals who fail to do what is required. The clerks may need to report on omissions, and possibly be given a training role.

4. The chief executive must make accountabilities clear, and clarify the terms of reference of the group – advisory, research or executive, for example – in relation to the manager's own agreed responsibility.

Process

Whether we use key result areas or tasks and standards, there is little scope to specify *how* the job holder achieves results – this could mean too much emphasis being put on quantitative output and concrete results and not enough on the quality of the process used. The latter is hard to define and often even harder to measure. Yet most healthcare professionals put much store by *the way* a person works. A nurse or occupational therapist performs well because she achieves results *and* displays a high level of process skills – she is caring, or sensitive, or reassuring, not just effective. It is worth bearing this in mind when we to start to write objectives.

Case Study
Setting Objectives for Staff

We will work through the imaginary case of Neil Kennedy, an F grade nurse in the NHS, to show how a work role statement can be used to identify key objectives. We will review his work role, then go through the process of setting these objectives. Later in this book (in Chapter 10), we shall show how his performance of one of them is reviewed. Initially, we will go through these stages:

1. reviewing changes in key result areas
2. identifying changes in assignments and projects

3.   identifying team contributions, and
4.   agreeing key objectives for the coming year.

By *key objectives* we mean priorities for the coming year, which can derive from any aspects of the work role, the assignments and projects he is undertaking, or his team contributions. As we only want a few key objectives, we will not be trying to set objectives for all the different aspects of Neil's work role. We will however be updating with him the things we require him to do. We also need to consider his personal developmental objectives, and will do so in the next chapter.

In discussing Neil's work role, his manager took account of some of the departmental objectives:

1.   To establish an improved form of care plan and ensure 95 per cent of patients' details are on stream by 1 June.
2.   To achieve three per cent savings on staffing costs over the year without loss of cover.
3.   To establish a planned schedule to replace outmoded equipment by 23 September.
4.   To investigate needs for support for relatives. To set up and evaluate pilot scheme using appropriate measures of effectiveness by 23 March.
5.   To ensure discharge procedures and information are ready for implementation of new computerised system by 1 January.

Neil's Work Role

We need not concern ourselves with the whole job description (see Figure 8.3). What is relevant here is that since last year he took responsibility for the infection control policies and for the supervision of students. His manager felt that the infection control responsibility could be transferred to someone else. The ward is not allocated as a training ward for students this year, so he is free to take on other key result areas.

Note that it was necessary to amend his overall responsibilities to ensure he had the authority to take decisions in some of the areas that were departmental priorities. The care planning task did not feature in his objectives, but the other four areas were seen as ones where he could contribute.

There was a need to make someone in charge of the implementation of the directorate equipment renewal policy in the department. At his personal development plan discussion recently, where Neil said he wanted to get more experience of management, it was agreed that he needed to become more involved with information systems, so it was felt that he could get involved with implementation of the new computerised discharge planning system.

Figure 8.3 Work role statement: Neil Kennedy, F Grade nurse manager

Changes in job responsibilities	Future key result areas:
Infection control	Transferred.
Student supervision	No longer required.
Information systems (*new responsibility*)	To implement and maintain operation of computerised ward information systems, ensuring quality standards are met and staff are competent
Staff allocation (*new responsibility*)	To achieve 3 per cent savings on staff costs without loss of cover.

Assignments and projects

Current	Future
To improve patient information on diabetes	To conduct survey of support needs of relatives by 30 June.
	To ensure equipment schedules are maintained and implemented to agreed standards.
	To ensure discharge procedures and information are ready for implementation of new computerised system by I January.

Team contributions

Current	Future
Blue team leader	Continuing.
Health and safety group	Continuing.
Care planning	To be member of care planning development team.

He agreed to take on responsibility for the systems in the ward, as the information manager had asked for a nominated individual from each ward. He was keen on being part of a team to improve care planning, and had relevant knowledge of this, having done a study of care planning as part of a course he completed recently.

He agreed to make this knowledge available to other members of the team and to give a presentation to the directorate. It was felt that he could help set up the scheme for support of relatives, by undertaking a survey into their needs. He was also made responsible for staff allocation in the ward so that he could show what he could do to make savings on staff costs. Figure 8.3 shows how these changes appeared on the work role statement. His job description was amended to take account of the changes in his job.

We are now able to agree some objectives, which are shown in Figure 8.4 (developmental objectives are covered in the next chapter).

Figure 8.4 Summary of key performance objectives: Neil Kennedy

---

Objective 1: *To implement staff allocation systems that will achieve 3 per cent savings on staffing costs over the year without loss of cover.*

Planned result/ measure – Total staff costs – target 3 per cent reduction. Criteria for assessing level of cover – to be agreed
Resources – Scope of existing staffing budget. One hour per week clerical help. Use of office and computer.
Support – Meet with manager monthly (plus help from finance, personnel).
Action plan – Agreed proposals within four weeks, then implementation.

Objective 2: *To establish a planned schedule to replace outmoded equipment by September 23.*

Planned result/measure – Schedule in place by target date. Target reduction in down time – 20 per cent.
Resources – Computer access.
Support – From Business manager, estates manager.
Action plan – Identify priorities; agree financial commitments; liaise with suppliers; devise schedule; implement; monitor; review.

Objective 3: *To investigate needs for support for relatives. To set up and evaluate pilot scheme using appropriate measures of effectiveness by 23 March.*

Planned result/ measure – Pilot scheme run and evaluated by target date. Evaluation by criteria – to be agreed.
Resources – Release one hour per week for research and liaison with university.

Support – Introductory course on counselling; specialist adviser.
Action plan – Research into needs; establish criteria; staff training; publicity; implement; evaluate.

Objective 4: *To ensure discharge procedures and information are ready for implementation of new computerised system by 1 January.*

Planned result/measure – Work complete by target date. Revisions to procedures agreed by all users. All identified users on line. All staff trained to level of competence. Data accuracy target 95 per cent. Data completeness 90 per cent.
Resources – Agreed budget; two hours per week release; staff release for training.
Support – Meeting with manager; information and training department.
Action plan – As per agreed corporate schedule.

Summary

The main purpose of job descriptions is to indicate accountabilities, and to specify overall job purpose and particular standing or ongoing responsibilities. Responsibilities can be described in terms of key result areas (useful when setting objectives) or, alternatively, as key tasks (which lends itself to standard setting). Simple jobs may suit this format better.

It is useful to review key result areas for each staff member in relation to departmental objectives. Work role statements may be devised to help allocate key objectives. They combine in one document: key result areas; key tasks; required competences; projects and assignments and required team contributions.

When creating a work role statement, we specify what the person does under these headings, and update this at regular intervals. This is done by reviewing changes in key result areas and identifying changes in assignments projects and team contributions.

We can use this updated statement to discuss and agree a small number of key objectives for the coming year. We do this by identifying key priorities (for the period in question) from any aspects of the work role. We do not attempt to set objectives for *all* aspects of the work role.

Chapter 9

Incorporating Learning Objectives

In this chapter we will be using the methods developed in previous chapters to create a personal development plan, the final piece in the achievement plan jigsaw. We need to use some of the principles of continuous development as set out by Mumford (1991) and Harrison (1988) for example. In principle we can set learning objectives in the same form as performance objectives, as a separate process – although there are good reasons for linking the two.

Here again, we are looking at the creation of objectives separately from the appraisal and review processes. In practice they must be integrated.

We need some way of identifying learning needs and methods. Study the algorithms (shown in Figures 9.1 and 9.2), and the personal development plan (Figure 9.6). They are virtually self-explanatory, but one or two features require some further comment.

Principles of the Learning Model

We know from studies by Mumford (1991) that the work environment provides powerful and varied opportunities for learning and that learning is the joint responsibility of the manager and the individual. Individuals will differ in their preferred learning style. It is important to develop people's ability to manage their own learning.

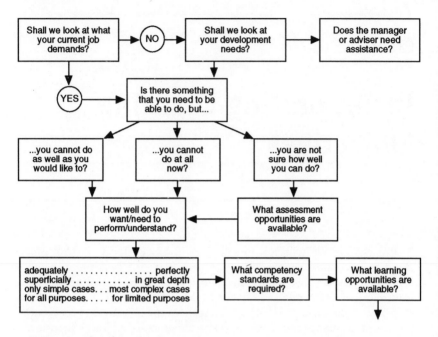

Figure 9.1 Identifying learning needs

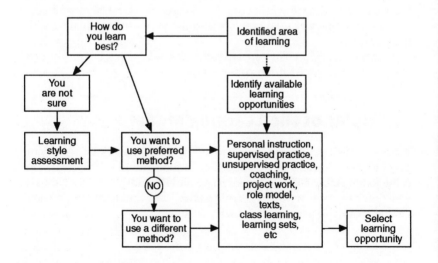

Figure 9.2 Identifying learning method

Competences

Lockett (1992) suggests that in developing any work role and progressing to new ones, different levels of competence may be required – from *threshold* competences which enable the individual to perform at a basic level only, to more *specialised* competences which give the individual greater range, or *generic* competences, which give the ability to operate competently by adapting to a wide range of situations. For example:

to interview patients on admission *(threshold* competence).
to conduct diagnostic interview *(specialised* competence).
to be able to use interviewing skills for selection, discipline, etc *(generic* competence).

It is important to be clear about the level and depth of competence required (see Figure 9.3).

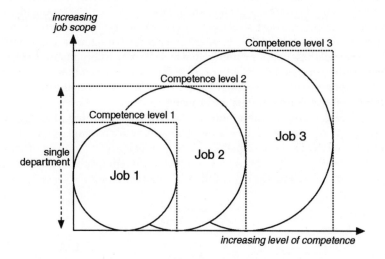

Figure 9.3 Job progression on existing competences. As people's competences grow, they are able to take on progressively bigger jobs, eventually needing to move outside the current department. Ideally, full competence in one post provides the threshold level of competence for the next. As people progress they need to acquire more generic competences.

Competences required for particular jobs need to be identified and related to the individual's current level, capacity and aspirations. This will involve analysing operational tasks to define the competence requirements of each. With a little thought and help, the manager should be able to identify the hierarchies of competence required in the jobs with which he or she is familiar – but the manager may have difficulty in identifying the competences required for other jobs, and in making an objective assessment of potential.

For a start, development needs related to jobs in the future are often too generalised and remote to relate easily to current activities. There is also the 'Peter Principle' effect where performance in the current job may not be the appropriate indicator of performance in a more senior post. There are many examples of where talent has not been recognised, and the individual may have been slapped down for showing 'too much initiative' or not being willing to serve time in a post which is insufficiently challenging.

The manager may not be aware of the indicators of potential in more senior posts, and may not be able to give the right kind of support and guidance to the high-flyer. There is also the danger from the kind of manager who does not want to lose the services of good workers by having them promoted or seconded away from the department with no one to replace them. So there is a need to ensure that opportunities for development in the current post are fully utilised, and for policies which ensure no manager is penalised for allowing his or her staff the chance to develop.

The development opportunities that arise from working situations may need to be supplemented, where necessary, by programmes that offer longer-range learning objectives. In addition, the right kind of support for individual development must be available.

Kolb *et al.* (1974) drew attention to the stages in a learning process (see Figure 9.4). Any learning environment must allow for all stages to be taken up adequately. There is frequently a lack of time for reflection and discussion of learning in healthcare environments. Sometimes there is a lack of opportunity for the right kind of 'hands on' practice, too.

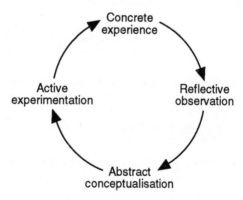

Figure 9.4 Kolb's learning cycle

Learning Styles

Honey and Mumford (1986) have offered a useful development of Kolb's cyclic model of the learning process. Their research indicated that the stages of the learning cycle can be used as the basis for the way people *prefer* to learn.

Activists involve themselves fully in new experiences. They are happy to be dominated by immediate experiences and are open-minded. They revel in short-term crisis fire fighting, tending to be bored with implementation and longer-term consolidation.

Reactors favour thorough collection and analysis of data about experiences, tending to postpone reaching definitive conclusions for as long as possible. They prefer observing other people in action; when they act themselves they do so with reference to a wider picture that includes the past and present, and others' observations as well as their own.

Theorists are detached, analytical and dedicated to rational objectivity. Their approach to problems is consistently logical. They prefer to maximise certainty and feel uncomfortable with subjective judgements.

Pragmatists are keen on trying out ideas, theories and techniques to see if they work in practice. They tend to be impatient with ruminating and open-ended discussions. They are essentially practical, down-to-earth people who like making practical decisions and solving problems.

A questionnaire to identify learning styles can be found in *The Manual of Learning Styles*. This enables us to match the learning opportunities to people's preferred style. It can also help individuals develop new styles and thus widen their access to learning opportunities. It is an example of the use of self-assessment which can be very valuable in promoting learning.

Harrison (1988) lists certain learning skills which should be actively developed in a working learning environment; these are: observation and reflection; analysis; creativity; decision making and problem solving; and evaluation.

Learning Opportunities

Among the opportunities available may be, for example:

personal instruction   studying role models
supervised practice   study of texts

unsupervised practice	class learning
coaching	learning sets.
project work	

Managers who are keen on continuous development must recognise the many learning opportunities that exist in work situations. In Chapter 4 we mentioned some of the things a manager could do to maximise workplace learning opportunities.

Managers may require assistance from outside: for example, in providing an objective assessment of the individual's development potential and giving appropriate career advice. They may need advice on competences outside their own experience, in conducting a competence analysis of a particular job, or in assessing an individual's current levels of competence.

There is likely to be some choice of learning opportunities available, and with the right information it will be possible to identify what is to be learned, to what level, to what means, with whose support, and within what time scale.

The Learning Objective

This can be stated in a similar form to that used for performance objectives, for example:

Learning objective: *To develop diagnostic interviewing skills.*
Planned outcome/standard – to conduct diagnostic interviews of relatives' needs for support to defined standards by the end of July.
Learning methods – coaching, role play; study; supervised practice.
Learning resources – purchase texts; use of work opportunities.
Support – from manager as coach.
Action plan – study; set success criteria; supervised role play; practice; assessment.

Links with Performance Objectives

Note the link here with the third performance objective (page 125). In Neil's case there are other performance objectives that offer opportunities to meet learning needs; for example, in information technology and budgeting. We can construct an achievement plan where learning and performance objectives are brought together, and given equal weight.

Traditionally performance objective-setting and personal development plans have been treated quite separately in appraisal schemes. Why is their integration being stressed here? Quite simply because learning objectives are universally neglected. Research in the NHS shows that personal development plans are often ignored in the IPR appraisal process. Learning objectives should have the same status as performance objectives. We also need to acknowledge learning and development aspects of performance objectives, and make best use of the learning opportunities at work. This integration should happen in practice as well as on paper.

For instance, it is useful to offer people opportunities to review their learning experience in working towards all their objectives. This can usefully be done in a learning set where peers can learn from each other and develop their ability to 'learn how to learn'. Figure 9.5 shows how the links can be made.

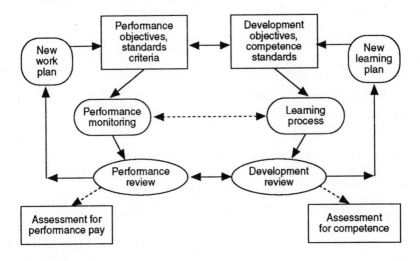

Figure 9.5 Links between performance and learning objectives

Personal Development Plans

If you wish to keep a separate record for personal development purposes – and this has some merit if you are dealing with specialised professional or career development – you can make personal development plans (see the example in Figure 9.6). This is helpful if you want to record and monitor the individual's longer term development needs.

Personal Development Plan   NAME: _____

1. Development in current post/development within department/career development*

2. Development need identified

3. Development objective (stating standard or outcome required)

4. Development action plan: how will the need be met (describe learning opportunities and milestones)

5. Time scale

6. What the staff member is required to do

7. What the manager is required to do

8. Requirements from others

9. Means of assessment

10. Notes on progress and outcomes

11. Included in portfolio?

12. Scope for application and consolidation of learning

13. Agreed by: _____ Date: _____

*Delete as appropriate (refer for specialist advice where necessary).

Figure 9.6 Example of a personal development plan

Going Further

Where individuals are felt to have the capability of progression in their careers, it will be necessary to offer them learning opportunities outside the department. Although there is obvious scope and demand for formal education, self-managed learning can be very effective.

Peer-based learning sets have been used at Roffey Park and elsewhere to help individuals develop learning plans and contracts with the group members, starting with the now familiar review questions:

- Where am I now?
- Where do I want to get to?
- How do I get there?
- How will I know when I've got there?

The development of the answers to these questions, aided by other members of the group, will enable learning objectives and criteria to be established. A learning plan is established which in the Roffey Park model incorporates peer assessment.

The Achievement Plan

We have now reached the stage where we can bring together performance and learning objectives to create the full achievement plan. It is important that the objectives are separable, and outcomes are separately assessable – but the processes can 'cross over' as depicted in Figure 9.5. We do not need to fill in any more forms, however!

We have agreed the person's performance objectives or standards (using the work role statement) and we have also derived learning objectives in a similar form, ie:

- Details of key (performance or learning) objectives or standards to be achieved.
- Time span required for completion of objectives or reaching standards.
- Agreed resources to be made available.
- Achievement outcome measures.
- Action plans, showing milestones.
- Authority, support and training requirements.

Details of all standards or objectives to be achieved must emerge from discussion and agreement during the initial appraisal phase. It is a good idea to ask the appraisee to propose some of the standards or objectives (no more than six) which will then be developed in discussion with the manager. A separate meeting will probably be required to draw up and agree the achievement plan. The objectives should be monitored and reviewed jointly in a later part of the appraisal process.

It may be that some assessment of the extent to which these objectives have been achieved forms the basis of a performance related pay scheme. In this case the manager needs to be aware of the conditions of the scheme and how achievement will be measured.

Summary

The work environment provides powerful and varied opportunities for learning; which is the joint responsibility of the manager and the individual. Individuals will have different preferred learning styles, and it is important to develop people's ability to manage their own learning.

Competence models are useful where they are specific enough to relate to actual work requirements. The levels of competence are *threshold, specialised,* or *generic.* Competences need to be identified and related to the individual's current level, capacity and aspirations.

The manager may need help and support in allowing staff development opportunities; these may need to be supplemented, where necessary, by programmes that offer longer-range learning objectives.

Managers should be aware of a range of learning opportunities available inside and outside the workplace, for example: personal instruction; supervised practice; unsupervised practice; coaching; projects; studying role models; study of texts; class learning; learning sets. Learning objectives can be stated in a similar form to that used for performance objectives.

An achievement plan is a statement of what the manager and member of staff have agreed to achieve during the period in question (normally one year) and includes (for performance and development):

Details of key objectives or standards to be achieved.
Time span required for completion of objectives or reaching standards.
Agreed resources to be made available.
Achievement outcome measures.
Action plans showing milestones.
Authority, support and training requirements.

Performance and learning objectives can both be expressed in this form, but it may be helpful to have a personal development plan, which can relate to longer-term development objectives.

Chapter 10

Performance Review Examples

In Chapter 9 we created an achievement plan and we will now use the review of this to illustrate some practical tactics managers can use in a formal review of performance. In this chapter we also consider some other cases and how to deal with them.

Review of Neil's Achievement Plan

Neil Kennedy's full objectives are described in Chapters 8 and 9. Before the formal review, the manager had followed up Neil's progress several times in informal review meetings. There were no major problems, except in the objective concerned with reducing the costs of staffing cover (objective 1).

The manager knew this would be testing, involving as it did a difficult target and requiring a range of skills to be employed, which included financial analysis, service planning, negotiation and presentation skills. Since Neil had ambitions to be a manager, this was a useful assignment, where the learning aspects were as important as the performance aspects. I concentrate here on how the manager handled the performance review of this objective.

Before the meeting, the manager brought together all the statistical data she had available on staffing costs throughout the year and all the details of plans that had been agreed at previous meetings, including the achievement plan and notes of the personal development discussion from the previous year. She had written reminders of all the relevant outcomes.

She reminded herself what *she* wanted for the department from the project, and the standards of work that she wanted Neil to achieve, as well as the learning he should have got from it. She asked Neil to undertake some self-assessment for development purposes.

She had briefly spoken to the finance department and staff in her department to get their views of the project. She did not ask them to appraise Neil's performance but to give their reaction to the project and the demands made on them. The manager needed this kind of 'soft' information, as well as the hard facts on achievement of output targets. She was interested in how Neil had managed the project, not just the results. It had been agreed with Neil previously that people would be asked to make evaluations of his work, and Neil was asked to make a point of mentioning this to people early on.[1] (See the commentary below for notes.)

The manager would admit some negative feelings about Neil's work – that he was sometimes inclined to neglect detail and be rather dismissive of criticism, and that he was not ready yet for promotion, although he felt he was. She got on well with him, but did not like his occasional flippancy. She tried to put out of her mind any prejudices there might be about him, in order to do justice to his actual performance and provide unbiased guidance.[2]

After careful consideration she identified a number of facts and re-corded her preliminary impressions. These were starting points for the discussion. She was ready to consider any new information or change her impressions, if there were good reason to do so.

The Facts

The target had not been achieved – the overall reduction had dropped to 1.9 per cent over the year, but had been as high as 4.1 per cent up to January.

Some staff had been surprised that Neil had been given the project, and were not initially cooperative. There was some adverse reaction to attempts to cut cover when the staff felt they were overstretched. There had been examples of bad morale when shift patterns had been changed at short notice. Some staff did not appear to know what was happening or why, and some resented working with people they did not get on with. The personnel manager said that Neil had not contacted him as expected, and an accountant said that he gave Neil a lot of data, but 'he tended to do his own thing with it' and he was not sure Neil understood the way seasonal fluctuations were built into the budget.

First Impressions and Areas for Further Investigation

- Neil had initially started well and achieved some savings. Something had gone wrong in January that Neil had not foreseen. He may not have anticipated a problem or followed it through adequately. Did he lose interest? Were there other pressures that he was finding hard to manage?[3]
- The lack of support by staff was a little worrying. It could indicate that Neil had neglected to communicate his intentions and win people's support, or a lack of skill in this area.[3]
- He might need better understanding of financial analysis.
- Neil neglected some areas, especially the idea of getting part-timers to do extra shifts. Why was this? This neglect of parts of the job was true of some other objectives as well.[4]

Tactics

The manager planned to base the review on the review questions:[5]

What went well – and why?
What did not go well – and why?
If you had to do it again what would you do differently – and why?
What action do you need to take?

Neil would be asked to undertake a self-assessment[6] to begin with, then the manager could make her views known at each stage. Initially it would be on the level of sharing information, leading into a diagnosis where useful.

Neil was aware of the failure to reach the target. Because they had discussed the project during informal appraisal sessions[7] the manager was aware of Neil's assessment of the project. The manager asked whether Neil felt that her support was sufficient and of the right kind.[8] They discussed the need to allow Neil to make decisions, even if they didn't always work out. This meeting provided the opportunity to sum up the achievements, shortfalls and learning needs. Some of the others' evaluative comments came as a surprise to him. He said:

Perhaps I took some people's cooperation for granted, or I didn't ask myself the right questions!

Neil felt that the target was not really achievable, and that the workload pressures in January were so unpredictable that they tended to scupper any plans.

If you felt that way, I guess you felt you couldn't do much more, then?[9]
That's right! I think I lost interest at that point.
I noticed that you had a similar reaction in the third objective.[10]
I suppose so. If you've got a lot to do you tend to concentrate on what you can make progress with.
Yes, but can we look at what you might have been able to do in that situation?[11] Did you have all the information necessary?
More than I could cope with.
But did you understand how the finance department models seasonal fluctuations?
I think so.
How did you use it, then?
I put more resource into January's staffing.
I think you'll find that had already been done by finance.
Oh![12]
Ok, was there any other factor that you might have been able to work on?[13]
I can't think of any.
What about the use of part-timers to cover for short periods by extending their hours?
Well, they didn't seem very interested.
Did you try to influence them?
No, because when I asked them I was just exploring possibilities.
It might have made a difference.
I accept that.
Could you have communicated the message better?
I think you are a bit harsh if you are saying I lack communication skills – I can show you that it is a strong point of mine.
I didn't make quite such a generalisation.[14] I was asking you if you felt that there was any way you could have prevented the reaction by staff?
Give them more time?
Yes. What about the way you communicated?[15]
I think that personal communication would have been more effective – but I find it hard to lean on people.
So perhaps there is a skills development need there? [15]
I didn't think I had a problem there.
Now we've explored it a bit, can you see ways in which you could have improved the way you did things?[16]

Some discussion ensued about contingency planning, the importance of follow through, and how staff commitment could have been fostered with more planning, identifying staff concerns and taking a more positive attempt to influence the staff concerned. After this Neil felt a bit deflated.

Don't get things out of proportion. That wasn't any easy task, and it was the only one where you failed to come up with the goods completely.

Shall we look at how I can help you build on what you've learnt and maybe put right any areas of weakness?[17]

Finally, his manager made a summary of the achievements and shortfalls and the development needs that had been identified. Neil was able to agree to the manager's summary of his achievements, and to the proposals for his future development. The summary looked like this:

Neil Kennedy has made a very useful contribution to the work of the department this year. All but one of his objectives have been met in full. The only shortfall, in a very difficult managerial objective, was fairly slight. While acknowledging his efforts, we have agreed that some development needs remain and that his experience of management should be given continued scope to develop in the coming year, through objectives that will develop skills in communication, planning and financial analysis. I would estimate that he will be ready for promotion in one to two years.

Neil wrote:

I feel I have made considerable progress this year and accept my manager's verdict. I am grateful for the opportunities for development. I am keen to prove that I will be ready for promotion before the suggested time.

Commentary

1. Note the sensitivity required in setting up and getting permission to gather this kind of information.
2. It is a good idea to list facts and impressions separately.
3. Keep in mind alternative explanations – explore precise causes in the interview.
4. A possible causal link here. Try to relate things wherever possible.
5. This technique is powerful; it generates *ownership* and has wide applications for development.
6. Try to introduce *self-assessment* wherever possible.
7. Much will have been covered already, so aim for *no surprises* at this stage.
8. The review here is *two-way*. Did the manager provide the right kind of support?
9. This is a reflective type of question, which helps develop an unthreatening line of probing.
10. Linking again.
11. Good confronting technique here.
12. At this point Neil realises that his understanding was faulty.
13. Use of exhaustive probe question.
14. It is important to correct misunderstandings, probably with an emotional cause.
15. Good use of direct questions.

16. Inviting Neil to come up with the answer.
17. An attempt to rebuild confidence and offer support.

Case Studies

Here we discuss the approach required in appraising individuals who present particular problems. Readers may like to consider their own responses before reading my suggestions.

Case 1
This individual is a good friend of the appraiser, and finds it hard to take the process seriously. The manager finds it hard to make criticisms. There is room for improvement in performance.

Case 2
This person is very unassertive. She is very unforthcoming and tends to accept what is being said without comment. She wants to get out of the room as soon as she can.

Case 3
This person wants a quiet life before taking retirement. They have no interest in development, and a rather cynical attitude to everything. Performance is adequate. You have evidence that this person is not putting in much effort at the moment, and is trying to cover that up.

Case 4
This individual is very keen to learn, and expects too much from the boss. She performs promisingly, but she is not as good as she thinks she is.

Case 5
This person is defensive and unpopular. She will tend to put the blame for any shortcomings on other people or the system. It is hard to assess her performance, and unwillingness to acknowledge development needs makes it hard for her to be helped to develop.

Case 6
Here is someone you don't have a very good relationship with. There is little rapport, and in the past there have been misunderstandings. You are not sure why.

Case 7
This person is older and has a lot more experience than the manager, and lets the manager know it. Her performance is inflexible – she resists change.

Case 8
This person is a serious under-performer. Her health record is poor and when she is present she does not perform well. You have considered disciplinary action.

Case 9
This person disagrees with assessments made of her and claims she has evidence to prove it.

Suggestions for Dealing with the Cases

Case 1
Tell the person what you have to do. Give them something to study beforehand which they have not seen before and which makes them think about their role and development. Make sure the setting is not too informal, and is free from interruptions. Use the 'buddy' relationship in discussion development, and ensure there is a two-way commitment. Involve another person, though, if it helps, eg, in a mentor role, or to give a more detached assessment. Be normally assertive about what you want from the person.

Case 2
Make her feel very welcome. Make sure you talk reassuringly to begin with and explain that it is important for you to hear her opinions. Spend time discussing the things she does well. If necessary mention her lack of assertiveness and say that you want to help her improve and explain that this is an important objective for both of you. Ask open questions. Give encouragement to her to make initiatives for objectives, and do not let her leave until she has responded and come up with some proposals.

Case 3
Find out what the person will find motivating. Signal that you are aware of the person's low-key contribution (check out that the individual is also aware). Discuss the difficulty for you of having someone who wants to take a back seat. Recognise any thwarted need for recognition. Make it clear that the person must be prepared to take some responsibility and that you are prepared to support a retirement application only if the person is willing to make some effort in the mean time.

Case 4
Use supportive confrontation here. Suggest appraisal methods that will support her learning. Establish clear cut criteria, and take her achievement targets initially at face value. Get her interested in self-managed learning. Set difficult assignments. Do not over commit yourself to training and support, but be prepared to meet her regularly – or find a mentor.

Case 5
Listen to what she has to say and try to understand why she thinks as she does. Note any genuine causes of complaint. The problem may be a lack of confidence.

Decide whether this is the cause of her behaviour, or whether she has learned to be manipulative with management. Build confidence in your intentions. Provide incentives for her to become more open. Encourage her to accept responsibility herself. Make clear what she has to achieve and ensure that she has objectives which give her control. Try to get her views on how she would like to be assessed. Follow up any real grievance and arrange to come back to her soon.

Case 6

Use the first meeting to talk with the person and get to know her interests and attitudes a little better. Listen carefully, and try to identify things she says that you *can* work with. It may be that your relationship is never going to be a warm one, but it should be based on a very clear contract between you, even if this is a rather formal one. Make efforts to develop the relationship outside the meeting.

Case 7

Listen to what she has to say. Explain the criteria and how they have been interpreted. Ask her for data to support her position. Recognise her experience, and say you need to be able to use it in the department. Make it clear at the same time that you have responsibility as manager, and that you do expect her to set high standards. Offer her an updating programme (Retirement, transfer, or a part-time role may be the coward's option!)

Case 8

If necessary, check out any health or other major problems. Give a clear indication of the standards you require, and provide hard evidence of the things that are unsatisfactory. Make your concern clear. Explain that appraisal is not a disciplinary measure: it is based on the premise that people will be able to achieve an acceptable level of performance. If she falls visibly short of the minimum then disciplinary action may result. Neither of you will want that, and so use the appraisal opportunity to make clear what is required and follow up the agreement closely. Offer what help you can (training, counselling, etc, if this is likely to help).

Case 9

Listen to what she has to say. Explain the criteria and how they have been interpreted. Ask her for data to support her position. If you disagree, and are right, stick to your guns.

Summary

Before the formal review, the manager had followed up the person's progress several times in informal review meetings. Before the meeting, the manager brought together all the statistical data and details of plans agreed previously, including the achievement plan and notes of the personal development discussion from the previous year. She had written reminders of all the relevant outcomes. She reminded herself what *she* wanted of the department from the project, and the standards of work that she wanted the person to achieve, as well as the learning he should have got from it.

She asked him to undertake some self-assessment for development purposes. She had briefly spoken to the finance department and staff in the department to get their views of the project. She did not ask them to appraise his performance but to give their reaction to the project and the demands made on them.

She was interested in how he had managed the project, not just the results. He had agreed previously that people would be asked to make evaluations of his work, and he was asked to make a point of mentioning this to people early on. After careful consideration the manager identified a number of facts and recorded her preliminary impressions.

During the meeting she used the following questions to initiate the review discussion:

What went well – and why?
What did not go well – and why?
If you had to do it again what would you do differently – and why?
What action do you need to take?

The appraisee was asked to share his self-assessment. The manager made her views known at each stage. Initially it would be on the level of sharing information, leading into a diagnosis where useful.

After extensive discussion the manager made a summary of the appraisee's achievements and shortfalls and the development needs that had been identified. The appraisee was able to agree to the manager's summary of his achievements, and to the proposals for his future development that had been proposed.

Further case studies drew out the performance review process.

Chapter 11

Performance Related Pay

Performance related pay (PRP) can be defined as:

> that part of the financial, or financially measurable, reward to a person which is linked directly to individual, team or company performance.

Note that the basis of the reward could be team or company performance, as well as individual performance.

How Effective is Pay as a Reward?

Vicky Wright (1991) says that:

> 'If people are in organisations where managers are adopting styles which are strongly achievement oriented, what can be the justification if one of the most potent communicators of values in the organisation (ie, pay) is not in accord with all other communications?'

She also acknowledges some problems in introducing it. Michael Armstrong (1994) states:

> 'Recent research on motivation has confirmed that intrinsic interest in a task – the sense that something is worth doing only for its own sake – typically declines when someone is only given external reasons for doing it... it can build an insatiable appetite for monetary reward'.

Things that healthcare staff find rewarding appear to be patient satisfaction, recognition, the work itself (especially where it involves patient contact and use of skills), responsibility, opportunity for development, recognition, autonomy, and successful team work. There is plenty of evidence that people who have chosen to work in the NHS are not people primarily motivated by money.

Heery (1994) confirms the strength of intrinsic motivation. He says that such commitment is 'neither generated by managers nor easily manipulated through management techniques'. He suggests that the introduction of performance pay in the public sector will be demotivating where people receive negative feedback on performance. Others will react by adopting a more calculative approach to their employment, as they will interpret the message that they are no longer to be trusted to maintain their own standards. Martin (1994) quotes research that implies that when money is a motivator there is a degradation of the meaning of work and an impact on standards – with corners being cut and people choosing to do the minimum necessary. In other words, the provision of *extrinsic* motivation undermines the *intrinsic* motivation do a job well. This may be because the requirements have effectively changed, but also because people who see themselves doing things for the money feel they no longer have any pride in their work, and take less pleasure in doing it.

New Opportunities to Link Pay to Performance

Traditionally, pay in the NHS has been based on a number of factors, related to competence, extra duties, hardship, and length of service, rather than performance. Payment has largely been made on the basis of grade definitions, for size of job undertaken and competences. This sets the basic pay level. Many pay systems included a short incremental scale based on length of service for each grade band. Further progress would depend on promotion or regrading of the post. Small extra duty, hardship and skills allowances have been common. Apart from productivity schemes set up locally for ancillary workers (portering, cleaning and catering staff), and merit pay for hospital consultants, pay was not based on performance until the advent of PRP for senior managers in 1986. This provided for cumulative pay increments to be awarded for high performance against objectives, set and assessed annually.

With the advent of NHS Trusts from 1991 onwards, offering staff local non-Whitley contracts of employment, progressively more encouragement has been given to the creation of local pay scales, which often contain linked spine points intended to replace the complicated pattern of allowances and increments. Staff are now allocated to a particular spine point based on job evaluation and influenced by market factors and, in some cases, personal negotiation. Where increments have been created between the spine points, this could allow in principle for an element of pay for performance or acquisition of competence.

The pay structures do therefore exist for individual PRP as well as for the payment of bonuses to particular groups of staff for performance. The latter raises questions about how the performance of different groups can be fairly compared. If business plan targets are used for instance, there are clear differences in difficulty of achievement, and control.

There are also debates about whether the PRP should be given as a single one-off annual bonus, or consolidated into pay. The latter is proving expensive, particularly on a cumulative basis, and many Trusts are now dropping the idea.

Human resource managers have emphasised the principle of linking pay and performance for these reasons:

- If pay motivates staff, then the opportunity to enhance performance through pay is one that should not be ignored, as it has been in the past.
- If pay enhancement does not relate to performance at all, but relates to other factors, then we may be wasting money rewarding time served, or providing generous sick pay, neither of which improve performance.
- PRP could be self financing if the right performance targets are set. At any rate it provides a means of starting to value human assets in business terms.
- PRP should attract and retain high performers if they are motivated by the chance to earn more.
- Stressing factors other than performance encourages the retention of non-performers – ie, people who remain for sickness or pension benefits.
- Until now, local managers have had little control over pay levels, despite the fact that staff have constituted 70 per cent of their costs.
- It is a better way of gearing pay to a competitive market for staff. In the past the NHS has suffered from uncompetitive salaries and inflexible, unattractive incremental scales.
- The measurement systems required for PRP will indicate the distribution of performance within the organisation, and allow new strategies for improvement and intervention to be devised to improve it.
- PRP helps create a performance-oriented culture and give the right signals to staff that their performance will be rewarded.

On the other hand, there is a down side to the PRP strategy:

- Pay has to motivate. There is plenty of evidence that, for many health-care staff, intrinsic motivation is far more important.
- Quantitative measurement has to be possible. Much healthcare work is not easily amenable to performance measurement.

- There is a danger that PRP will depend on the measurement of short-term outputs which support management productivity targets while longer-term qualitative outcomes are ignored.
- Performance-orientation supported by cash rewards may be alien to care staff and is a malign and damaging influence. It signals that managers are in control, not the professional practitioner.
- The assessment of performance must be fair and objective. This depends largely on the design of the system and the abilities of raters.
- Rewards must be allocated to those responsible for the achievement of performance. Where attribution is not clear then the allocation of rewards may be inappropriate. This raises the question of a team or individual basis for reward.
- Employees must believe that improved performance will be rewarded and these rewards must be large enough to be valued.
- The reward must not come at an unacceptable cost. Staff may feel that their gain is someone else's loss – or the objectives set may involve conflict with other important values, eg, achieving increased output but increasing the risk to patients.
- Introduction of PRP may reduce the level of trust and damage team building.
- The payout is always partly driven by economic success. In commercial companies, market circumstances have meant that even for high performers, no payout is possible in lean years. This has damaged motivation. The ability of the NHS to put up the cash is questionable.
- The introduction of pay to the performance appraisal process could prevent open discussion, require attribution of failure (however unreasonably) and stifle the development process.

Research Findings

Research shows that performance pay is anything but a success story. Here is a summary of some recent research:

In a study of 598 private-sector organisations, only 11 per cent of organisations believe merit pay to be effective; few employees could see a link between pay increases and performance – even when seen as fair they did not help improve performance. *Wyatt, IDS Top Pay Unit Review, No. 120, February 1991.*

An Inland Revenue study showed that staff were not averse to PRP in principle, but in practice felt it to be unfair – its application undermined morale and caused jealousies between staff.

A study in BT indicated that the payment of bonuses demotivated those who did not receive it more than it motivated those who did. Only 6 per cent of executives thought that PRP improved their performance. *Quoted by Armstrong (1993).*

In the NHS in 1991 a study by the IHSM showed that those managers who received PRP thought it was motivating, but their motivation scores were significantly lower than those who did not receive it. They were less likely to agree that PRP increased trust or helped team building.

It is by no means implausible that the net motivational effect has been negative. *Richardson, R and Marsden, D, 'Does Performance Pay Motivate!' An Interim Report for The Inland Revenue Staff Federation, London School of Economics, 1992.*

Belief in merit pay's efficacy is based more on faith than hard evidence. *The Economist, 18 January 1992.*

If these studies are correct (and they all reach the same conclusion), the wide scale introduction of performance pay into the NHS will have, at best, no impact on individual and organizational performance, and at worse, will result in a decline in morale and motivation. *'Why Doesn't Performance Pay Work?', Health Manpower Management, 19 February 1993.*

After a US study on 163 firms the researchers concluded that pay and company financial performance are largely uncorrelated. *Berlet, KR and Cravens, DM, Performance Pay as a Competitive Weapon, London: Wiley, 1991.*

In a study of 856 organisations in the public and private sectors and representing 20% of the UK work force the IPM concluded that there was no correlation between the use of PRP and organisational performance. *Institute of Personnel Management, Performance Management In the U.K.: an analysis of the issues, London: IPM, 1992.*

The Politics of PRP

The Conservative Government's reforms of the NHS have introduced a competitive, market-driven approach to its management. PRP fits in with this philosophy and is also congruent with The Citizen's Charter with its emphasis on standards and value for money. It also believes that there should be a regular and direct link between pay and standards of service provided. We can add the managerial philosophy that it is possible to create a performance culture which achieves excellence in a competitive market by stimulating commitment and effort. Opponents of this philosophy maintain that public service professionals (who often work beyond the contractual requirement) bring a vocational commitment to their work which acts as a source of intrinsic motivation independently of any market discipline or management-driven culture.

Referring to nursing, Graeme Martin (1994) summarises healthcare service as: largely intangible; involving inseparable links between the producers (nurses); perishable (the service cannot be stored); and variable (because the producer-consumer interactions involved are unique). These conditions are not ones that offer any clear-cut basis for performance measurement.

The trade union response has been to seek to control the impact of performance pay schemes by negotiating a reduction in the subjectivity and unfairness through limiting management discretion and introducing better assessment criteria, monitoring and appeals systems. They are also concerned about the burgeoning evidence that gender discrimination can occur. Alimo-Metcalfe (1994) quotes research showing that twice as many men as women got top ratings on PRP in the NHS.

The current priorities of the NHS would lead us to expect that the objectives and performance indicators adopted will be concerned with cuts – which are easier to measure than benefits. Less tangible, longer-range outcomes will be ignored. Politically this will be seen as increasing managerial control over services, and this could be detrimental to quality and innovation. The combination of PRP for some and redundancy for others is not a happy one.

Alimo-Metcalfe (1994) is in no doubt about what the verdict on PRP should be:

> Policies of PRP kill the desire to challenge, take risks, experiment and collaborate. They embody an ideology which results in a preoccupation with the individual's task rather than the organisation's aims. PRP focuses on the short term; divides the work force; creates disaffected staff; encourages adversarial relations and violates the logic of co-ordinated and co-operative systems and leads to conflict, defensive behaviour and opposition to risk taking and innovation – overall, a formidable barrier to adapting to change.

She recommends chief executives to forget about PRP and to concentrate instead on encouraging staff development.

Current and Future Developments

There is evidence of a return to group bonus schemes, largely discredited in the past as a means of raising basic pay levels rather than productivity in ancillary workers. This time they will be designed to have more impact on performance, but this could lead to a continuation of the fragmentation of healthcare workforces into professional and non-professional groups with different bases of payment. It also assumes that there is some higher staff productivity to be achieved – and many staff claim to be working at the limits of their capacity already. We are also seeing pay scales that allow pay increments for acquisition of competences. This will fit well with the introduction of care workers, but can often lead to individual demands for opportunities to go further on the NVQ trail than the organisation can afford – hence bringing a certain disillusionment.

Encouraged by the government, many public sector organisations are rushing to introduce individual PRP based on achievement of objectives, confident, no doubt, they can succeed where others have failed. Home-wood Trust claims to have got it running, but it is not at all clear what benefits have been achieved. Derby City Hospital Trust is seeking to operate PRP on the basis of 'professional contribution' once they have sorted out the criteria. One suspects that there will be much public relations activity and little impartial evaluation while the area is receiving such strong government backing.

Looking into a crystal ball, there may be three possible outcomes. One is the staking-out of areas of performance pay that are within the domain of management priorities, such as cost reductions, efficiency savings, and meeting throughput targets. Hence a proportion of pay may be based on achieving these, with little impact on clinical standards. This might be most acceptable on a group basis, with directorates, for instance, achieving bonuses for surpassing contract requirements. Staff may see this as management compensating them for achieving results under pressure. The difficult area of performance pay for clinical work would remain untouched.

The second outcome could be a transformation of the basis of performance pay through professional collaboration, with meaningful clinical outcomes being included in the package of performance measures. This means having clinical performance indicators that clinicians find acceptable. Doctors will be the 'litmus' group here, and if history is anything to go by, they would never accept the management performance agenda unconditionally.

The third outcome would be to abandon PRP as a failed experiment, replacing it, perhaps, with a culture of achievement based on the development of staff and service quality. This approach could be based on extrinsic rewards that are not financial, but that would be valued by healthcare staff, such as opportunities for professional development.

Employment contracts have already begun to show the influence of market-driven pay scales, with basic pay and incremental scales relating to the local market rather than to nationally bargained rates. Despite pressure from the NHS executive, there have been simplifications of Whitley terms rather than a total rejection of them. In many cases this incorporates payment for the achievement of required competences.

Summary

PRP is that part of the financial, or financially measurable, reward to an individual which is linked directly to individual, team or company performance. The basis of the reward could be team or company performance, as well as individual performance. People who have chosen to work in the NHS may not be primarily motivated by money; they may prefer to work for patient satisfaction, recognition, or opportunity for development.

Traditionally, pay in the NHS has been based on a number of nationally agreed factors, related to competence, extra duties, hardship, and length of service, rather than performance. Since 1991, local pay scales have appeared, with linked spine points to allow an element of pay for performance or acquisition of competence to be included.

Enthusiasts argue that linking pay to performance locally is necessary in a competitive environment, and that it supports a performance-oriented culture. Sceptics maintain that it is inappropriate for the NHS staff, who will not be motivated by money. Fair comparison of the performance of different occupational groups may be problematic, and there are difficult decisions about whether the PRP should be given as a single one-off annual bonus, or consolidated into pay; whether it is based on group or individual performance and whether it should relate to the achievement of business targets or to clinical performance as well. There are difficulties in providing an appropriate level of reward and in measuring performance without affecting motivation. Research elsewhere suggests that PRP in the NHS will have no impact on individual and organisational performance, and may result in a decline in morale and motivation.

To work, PRP requires a supportive culture, geared to agreed standards of performance, relationships of trust where employees' and employers' objectives coincide; a system of objective measurement and a willingness to accept ratings – and the competence to administer them effectively. Sufficient funding is required to enable worthwhile pay-outs to be made.

The system which finally predominates may offer staff compensation for achieving results under pressure, with the difficult area of performance pay for clinical work untouched by PRP. Alternatively, there could be a transformation of the basis of performance pay through professional collaboration, with meaningful clinical outcomes included in the package of performance measures. A third outcome would be an abandonment of PRP altogether, perhaps being replaced by a culture of achievement based on the development of staff and service quality.

Appendix I

Business Planning

Business planning is a process which describes how activities are to be matched to resources over a given period of time. It reviews current activity in some detail, outlines future goals, and expresses a strategy for achieving them. It should address short-term operational needs as well as longer-term strategic needs. Thus it should provide a link between corporate plans and service demands.

Without a business plan some key issues may be neglected, or the service may be wrong-footed when conditions change. While healthcare cannot be seen as merely a commercial enterprise, it is still necessary to make plans that are sound in exactly the same as if we were running a business.

In the past, service planning has often meant drawing up a development plan for a defined service area and attaching some costs. Business planning is different because it takes a more comprehensive view. It is concerned with what can be done with the resources available, and how future capability can be assured.

It is also the basis of planning services for some sort of market. The plan must certainly be driven as much by purchaser intentions and wants as by finance available. Assumptions about the environment in which a service operates have to be made explicit. There also needs to be some contingency planning to allow for change. It is likely to include a human resources and training plan and this provides scope for an agreed approach to performance management. For all this, accurate data are essential.

A typical set of headings found in a written business plan are:

1. An introduction.
2. A summary of the main aspects of the plan.
3. Service descriptions and profiles, including details of the organisation of services as well as activities, including teaching and research where appropriate.

4. A description of the market/s for these services.
5. Operational goals or objectives.
6. The operational plan. It is important here to include plans to increase capability as well as delivering the required volume of activity.
7. Notes on relationships with other service centres. It is important that the implications of one business plan on others are carefully considered.
8. Human resources and training plan.
9. A plan for quality assurance.
10. A financial plan, which may include budgets and cost breakdowns, service pricing and the capacity for increasing workload at marginal cost.
11. Details on how the plan is to be monitored.

Business Plan Co-ordination

The business plan is not self contained. Plans are likely to be more ambitious than corporate resourcing allows – hence some capacity for overview and revision is needed. There should be a phasing of business plans to ensure that 'front-line' Service Centres or Directorates publish very clearly their assumptions about 'back up' services like pathology laboratory tests and drugs, before the Pathology and Pharmacy business plans are drawn up. A good deal of negotiation and revision is likely before final plans are published. Nevertheless business planning strongly reinforces the Directorate as the cost and profit centre and reinforces its managerial role.

To summarise, the business planning process enables corporate and customer requirements to be interpreted and responded to. It also provides the means for collection of data and for open review of progress and the means for discussion of future goals.

Since it states specific agreed directorate goals and resources to be used, it can be made the basis for individual objectives setting and performance plans for both service activity, finance and human resources.

Appendix 2

Identifying Team Performance Requirements through Departmental Business Planning

Building Goals through Discussion

Here we show how a participative business planning process can be used to identify the goals of a department which is part of a larger directorate so as to create its own local 'business plan'. Thus the term 'business planning' refers just as much to a developmental process as to a written plan. Its creation can become a valuable process in itself. Creating a business plan together provides an ideal opportunity for a discussion of services with all the staff involved. Here is one way for the manager to address expectations and secure the commitment of staff at the same time. Quite often individual concerns and enthusiasms emerge which give the manager leads when it comes to discussing individual objectives and development plans.

Team Planning

The best way to start to develop a performance plan for a department is to set up business planning sessions which are highly participative and carefully planned to achieve this objective. Half a day is set aside for an entire team to meet and thrash out their team objectives. A plan for such an event is shown below.

Timing

If this exercise occurs *before* the directorate plan is drawn up and finalised, one may not be aware of all the goals and demands which will be imposed on the department from above, or know what resources are available. If, on the other hand, one waits until the 'bigger picture' becomes clear, the opportunity for influencing the wider process and getting a sense of ownership from staff may be missed. In practice, if resource assumptions and team objectives do not vary greatly from year to year, it is possible to start this process before the directorate business plan is drawn up, provided conservative assumptions are made about finance and that there is a concentration on issues that will bring savings or are self-financing. Team objectives having cost implications must be prioritised. What is produced must be assimilable into the directorate plan. The plan will need to be adapted later on when members of the team should be made aware of any changes in objectives and resources.

Collection of Information

Plans must be made to identify and collect what is required. Often information about attitudes and expectations is equally as important as hard activity and cost data. In the event of a performance shortfall, a diagnostic process is undertaken in order to ascertain where failure has occurred.

Use of SWOT Analysis

The popular SWOT analysis is a very good starting point for the review process. This means identifying *strengths, weaknesses, opportunities* and *threats*. For anyone not yet familiar with SWOT analysis, here is a brief guide.

Strengths are any aspects of the organisation which are seen as current assets. They may be quality, responsiveness, the commitment of staff, financial security, experience, etc. A *weakness* is the opposite – either something which could be improved, like poor reception facilities, or something that has to be lived with, like poor road access. An *opportunity* is something that could be taken advantage of in future – usually an external change that opens a door to do something new. A *threat* is something that could happen, against which one might need to take defensive action – a rival in the market, a potential loss of resources or good will, for instance. The premises being in a bad state of repair is a *weakness* if it impairs capacity or confidence, but it could be a *threat* if the hospital is falling apart or if people may stop coming because of it.

As many people as possible should compare views on these aspects, noting any information that is lacking. It will almost certainly lead to identifying priorities or to discussions about what needs to be done, immediately or in the longer term, to strengthen the position or exploit the opportunity.

I find SWOT analysis particularly useful when combined with a check on the expectations of customers. First identify *all* of them – this can be salutary. Then ask what each expects from you. It is powerful to pose questions like: 'What do they want?' 'What do they say about us?'

Try to put it in the words clients would actually use, and then work out some convincing replies! You may need to check what they *do* think.

It is not too difficult to develop appropriate team objectives from the priorities which emerge. If this is done annually, then it can be linked to the review of performance objectives for the department. It will be useful to identify different perceptions of where things are and what the future might hold. The subsequent discussion and consultation are used to build goals which everyone in the organisation can contribute to and support. This is both educational and unifying for all involved.

Business plan team objectives must be reflected in individual and team objectives. Some process of allocating responsibilities is necessary if the team objectives are to be achieved. The more such goals are developed jointly the wider will be the sense of ownership.

Linking the Planning Session to Performance Reviews

Service reviews, team reviews and individual performance reviews can be used to provide feedback on outcomes and on results of actions planned and taken. The service review might provide the starting point for developing the new business plan by reviewing the outcomes of the previous one. People should feel that there is a link between performance reviews of outcomes and the team business plan.

Case Study

This illustration is based on a series of annual meetings that took place with all the staff of a chiropody department. All the staff, including professionals and support staff, foot-care assistants, part-timers and full-timers were invited. The invitation made it clear that all aspects of the department's work would be discussed, including professional quality standards and development needs. Beforehand, some information on the previous year's performance was disseminated, and people were asked where they felt things had gone well and where they had not and to record their own personal feelings about working in the department if they wanted to. Some of this information was summarised and presented in the first, review section The manager led this session, with contributions from senior staff who had taken a particular interest in aspects of the work.

After discussion, where all the staff's ideas on required improvements were recorded, the manager responded to people's comments in the first session. She then gave a full picture of requirements for the coming year, which she had gained from talking to the directorate business manager and the chief executive of the Trust. She emphasised the difficult financial position, the growing market among GP fund holders, the reorganisation of the Trust and the need to improve professional quality standards in some areas. Next, the whole group looked at future needs, reviewing last year's SWOT analysis to see what had changed. Small groups looked at the expectations of key customers and staff, and sought to identify these. Where there was a need for more information or education, this was noted. A long list of requirements emerged from these groups, (see 'Exploration of key issues' in the list below) and these were arranged into smaller agendas. Groups were then formed to examine these. (Organising this was the hardest part of the day.) These groups were charged with the identification of priorities for the coming year. Each group made a presentation, specifying in as much detail as possible:

- problems requiring attention
- proposed team objectives
- related information and monitoring requirements.

One of the groups took a particular interest in professional standards and development. The manager, having thanked people for their contributions, then asked participants to say which of several interest or project groups they might be interested in joining, to develop the ideas further. (It was agreed that the basis for involvement would be payment for 50 per cent of the time involved.)

The manager then went away and sorted out the ideas, identifying the priorities and adding other things which she felt important. With the help of colleagues she was able to draw up a draft business plan on the basis of this. She also spoke to individuals to suggest they took leadership of particular projects. She already had the names of a nucleus of volunteer staff who subsequently made up teams to work on particular areas, whose terms of reference she stated.

This enabled her to agree individual and small team objectives a little later on. The manager never lost sight of the fact that she was the person who had to take the decisions at the end of the day. She controlled the way the projects were allocated, and decided their terms of reference. She provided leadership and welcomed participation. Throughout, the communication was open and there were opportunities to criticise. The response to this way of working was very positive indeed, and she was able to introduce many successful changes as a result.

Here is a summary report of the chiropody department team planning meeting:

I. Review of previous year's plans and achievements

1. *Reports by manager and senior staff to cover*
   Activity
   Quality
   Finance
   Staffing
   Staff Development
   Information
   Marketing and impact of new services
   Outcomes of agreed projects and research
   Requirements and likely resources for coming year.
2. *Discussions*
   What has been achieved?
   What has not been achieved?
   What could we have done better?

II. Priorities for the coming year

3. *Update of SWOT analysis*
4. *Identification of customer expectations*
   GPs
   patients
   staff
   Directorate
   Trust board
   Medical consultants
   Social services
   Government (The Patient's Charter, waiting list, etc)
5. *Exploration of key issues (in syndicate groups)*
   Maintaining services and income
   Expansion of service with GPs
   Maintaining quality issues
   Internal operation of department: policies and procedures
   Improvement of administrative support
   Standardisation of assessment clinic procedure.
   Case-mix management
   Patient plans, long- and short-term referrals
   Specific assessment requirements
   Meeting expectations
   Expansion of GP fund-holding
   Reorganisation of Community Care

6. *Syndicate groups report back with proposed team objectives, and problems to be resolved*
7. *Manager summarises team's overall team objectives and thanks people for their contributions*

III. Follow up
8. *Two weeks later, after further discussion with individuals, the manager identifies*
   Outline service plan team objectives and projects
   Outline professional development plan team objectives and projects
   Accountabilities
   Key measures/ monitoring/ evaluation and control.

Service Quality and Staff Development Plans

When planning at this level it is important that one's agenda includes the development of service quality and the identification of professional development needs. These areas are often looked at outside the context of business and service planning; as a result they are often thought of as separate activities, when in fact they should be integrated. This has several advantages: it enables quality issues to be stressed in current activities and in all proposed new developments. It integrates staff development activity with service development, so that they reinforce each other. Resources and opportunities for development can be identified. It ensures that both clinical and managerial goals and achievements are recognised – this integration contributes to a sense of professional purpose and breaks down the distinction between the two areas. Professional development programmes are seen as contributing to service outcomes and the manager is seen as giving some priority to professional issues. This helps involve in the planning process those staff whose main interest is clinical.

References and Further Reading

Alimo-Metcalfe, B (1994) 'The poverty of PRP', *Health Service Journal*, October.

Armstrong, M (1993) *Managing Reward Systems*, Buckingham: Open University Press.

Armstrong, M (1994) *Performance Management*, London: Kogan Page.

Blanchard, K, Zigarmi, P and Zigarmi, D (1985) *Leadership and the One Minute Manager*, London: Fontana.

Crosby, R (1992) *Walking the Empowerment Tightrope*, Pennsylvania, PA: Organization Design & Development Inc.

Drucker, P (1955) *The Practice of Management*, Maidenhead: McGraw-Hill.

Dutfield, M and Eling, C (1990) *The Communicating Manager*, London: Element Books.

Fletcher, CA (1981) 'The effects of performance review in appraisal: evidence and implications', *Journal of Management Development*, 5,3.

Fletcher, CA (1993) 'Appraisal: an idea whose time has gone?', *Personnel Management*, September.

Fowler, A (1990) 'Performance management, the MBO of the '90s?', *Personnel Management*, July.

Freemantle, D (1994) *The Performance of Performance Appraisal: An appraisal*, Superboss Ltd.

Handy, C (1989) *The Age of Unreason*, London: Business Books.

Handy, C (1993) *Understanding Organisation*, (4th edn), Harmondsworth: Penguin.

Harrison, R (1988) *Training and Development*, London: IPD.

Heery E (1994) 'Vocational workers or shirkers?', *Health Matters*, 19.

Heery, E and Warhurst, J (1994) *Performance Related Pay and Trade Unions: Impact and Response*, Kingston Business School Occasional Paper, August.

Herzberg, F (1966) *Work and the Nature of Man*, Manchester: World Publishing Co.

Honey, P and Mumford, A (1986) *The Manual of Learning Styles*, 2nd edn, Peter Honey.

Institute of Personnel and Development (IPD) (1992) *Performance Management in the UK: An analysis of the issues*, London: IPD.

(The Institute of Personnel Management (IPM) is now known as the Institute of Personnel and Development (IPD)).

Institute of Personnel and Development (1994) *Position Paper: People make the difference*, London: IPD.

Kolb, DA, Rubin, IM and McIntryre, J (1974) *Organisational Psychology – An experimental approach*, Hemel Hempstead: Prentice Hall.

Lockett, J (1992) *Effective Performance Management*, London: Kogan Page.

McGregor, D (1957) 'An uneasy look at performance appraisal', *Harvard Business Review*, 35.

Mair, N (1985) 'Three types of appraisal interview', *Personnel*, March.

Martin, G (1994) *Health Manpower Management*.

Maslow, A (1970) *Motivation and Personality*, London: Harper & Row.

Meyer, HH, Kay, E and French, JPR (1965) 'Split roles in performance appraisal', *Harvard Business Review*, 35.

Mumford, A (1991) in Neale, F (ed.) *The Handbook of Performance Management*, London: IPM.

Peters, T (1988) *Thriving on Chaos*, Basingstoke: Macmillan.

Peters, T and Waterman, R (1982) *In Search of Excellence*, London: Harper & Row.

Randell, G, Packard P and Slater, J (1984) *Staff Appraisal: A first step to effective leadership*, London: IPM.

Schein, E (1965) *Organisational Psychology*, (2nd edn), Hemel Hempstead: Prentice Hall.

Vroom, VH, (1964) *Work and Motivation*, Chichester: Wiley.

Wright, V (1991) in Neale, F (ed.), *The Handbook of Performance Management*, London: IPM.

Index